ART INTO POP

ART INTO POP

Simon Frith • Howard Horne

Methuen
London and New York

First published in 1987 by
Methuen and Co. Ltd
11 New Fetter Lane, London EC4P 4EE

Published in the USA by
Methuen & Co.
in association with Methuen, Inc.
29 West 35th Street, New York NY 10001

Printed in Great Britain by
Richard Clay Ltd, Bungay,
Suffolk

British Library Cataloguing in Publication Data
Frith, Simon.
Art into pop.
1. Art and music   2. Music, popular
(songs, etc.)—20th century—
History and criticism.
I. Title   II. Horne, Howard
780'.42   ML3470

ISBN 0-416-41530-X
ISBN 0-416-41540-7 Pbk

Library of Congress Cataloging in Publication Data
Frith, Simon
Art into pop.
Includes index.
1. Rock music—Great Britain—History and criticism
2. Art and music.   I. Horne, Howard, 1951-
II. Title.
ML3650.F74   1987   784.5'4'00941   87-11308

ISBN 0-416-41530-X
ISBN 0-416-41540-7 (pbk.)

I wasn't one of what we called the Popular Kids – the cheerleaders and the football players. I used to hang around with the ugly people in the art room.

Chrissie Hynde

CONTENTS

ACKNOWLEDGEMENTS

We'd like to thank:

Klaus Frederking for first commissioning us to write about art and pop.

Gill Frith, Angela McRobbie, Will Straw, Colin Painter and Mavis Bayton for criticism, information and advice.

Greil Marcus and Jon Savage, who've done more than anyone to help us make sense of the day-to-day issues raised by art/pop, for sharing their ideas and commenting on our own.

Larry Grossberg and Iain Chambers, without whose pioneering theoretical work this book would have been impossible, for the care and patience with which they read our initial draft and disagreed with our arguments.

Alan Williams for his photography.

The authors and publishers would like to thank the following for their kind permission to reproduce the photographs in this book:

ACKNOWLEDGEMENTS

Peter Blake for no. 8 (p. 59)
EMI Records for no. 7 (p. 57)
Harry Hammond for nos 13 and 15 (pp. 142 and 150)
Thelma McGough for no. 9 (p. 82)
Metro Pictures for nos 18 and 20 (pp. 158 and 160)
Penguin Books for no. 5 (p. 50)
Polydor Records for nos 3, 10, 11 and 16 (pp. 26, 91, 125, and 152)
Jamie Reid for no. 1 (p. 9)
The Royal College of Art for no. 4 (p. 45)
Chris Stein for nos 17 and 19 (pp. 157 and 159)
Virgin Records for no. 14 (p. 146)
ZTT Records for no. 2 (p. 23)

1
ART AND POP

We began this book with a commonplace observation and a simple hypothesis. The observation was that a significant number of British pop musicians from the 1960s to the present were educated and first started performing in art schools. The hypothesis was that its art school connections explain the extraordinary international impact of British music since the Beatles. In musicological terms the history of post-war pop remains a history of Afro-American sounds. What British musicians have added is style, image, self-consciousness – an *attitude* to what commercial music could and should be. This attitude has been influential even when a particular British genre (like punk) didn't actually sell records.

Our aim, then, was to examine how and why art schools got implicated in British pop music and to assess the effects of their art school experience on British pop musicians. But even in the early stages of this research it became clear that to approach pop this way was to challenge two of the fundamental assumptions of contemporary cultural analysis.

First, virtually all general sociological accounts of capitalist societies assume a clear distinction between 'high' and 'mass' culture, between the bourgeois world of fine arts, academic music, serious literature, etc., on the one hand, and the popular world of TV, the tabloid press, Radio 1 music, etc., on the other. Art schools cross these divisions in terms of both class and ideology; art school graduates are petit-bourgeois professionals who, as pop musicians, apply 'high art' skills and identities to a mass cultural form. To follow through what this means is to raise general questions about the high/mass cultural divide.

Second, our questions can only be answered by putting musicians themselves at the centre of the pop process. Embedded in the high/mass cultural distinction is the assumption that while high art meaning is derived from the artists themselves – from their intentions, experience and genius – mass cultural meaning lies in its function (to make money/to reproduce the social order). Recent linguistically based cultural theories, which have challenged the authority of high artists, have only thus confirmed the unimportance of pop producers – all that matters is the text; all that's needed to understand it is a rigorous textual reading. Mass cultural forms – advertisements, TV shows, Hollywood films, Top Ten records – are all subject to the same kind of literary critical analysis. This approach links Leavisites to poststructuralists, makes Barthes as dismissive of mass culture as any Scrutineer, and even when critics try to disentangle the 'productive forces' that structure a film or record they still read back from the text to its meaning.

The populist version of structuralism – semiotics for people who like pop music and read Biff postcards – finds the positive meaning of mass culture not in its making but in its use. Dick Hebdige's *Subculture*, for example, reclaims mass culture for art via the concept of style. Creativity, self-expression, protest come back into the picture – at the moment of consumption. Hebdige provides a suggestive account of how this works (and breaks out of the simpleminded subculture/working class equation of his Birmingham colleagues) but he retains the traditional art/commerce categories, with the artist-consumer (romantically symbolized by Genet) allowed brief moments of expressive defiance in the market place before being absorbed, once more, by mass fashion.[1] Under what conditions such gestures are possible, how consumers and producers relate in the manufacture of style remains unclear.

In the pop world itself, of course, musicians are taken very seriously. The star system works by making them publicly responsible for their own sounds; the sales apparatus of the music press, radio and television depends on the star interview, on the myth of individual production, which is why critical theorists have always dismissed the stars' significance.[2] The only sociological theory to investigate performers at all is the interactionist approach developed in the USA by Howard Becker. Becker's pioneering studies of jazz musicians in the 1950s have been applied to pop music by several of his students but the most important book for our purposes is his own *Art Worlds*. (H. Stith Bennett's *On Becoming A Rock Musician*, for example, describes an entrepreneurial career model that doesn't fit the British 'revolt into style'.) Our concern is how, in art schools, a particular tension between creativity and commerce is confronted and how pop music works as a solution. Becker addresses this tension in a variety of art settings and, in particular, shows how the notion of 'art' itself is constructed and maintained in social practice, under what circumstances mass culture becomes 'art', art becomes mass culture. It is certainly arguable that high culture is itself simply now a mass cultural myth, a category created by specific state and market forces, specific middle-brow mass media – museums and exhibitions, poster and 'classic' book publishers, TV shows and radio programmes. Becker reveals, illuminatingly, just how much work goes into ensuring art's 'autonomy'.[3]

Postmodernism

The term 'art rock' still carries the resonance of a particular form of late 1960s/early 1970s album music, but as John Rockwell makes clear in *The Rolling Stone Illustrated History of Rock & Roll*, the claim that underlay art rockers' experiments was that their compositions 'paralleled, imitated, or were inspired by other forms of "higher", more "serious" music.'[4] 'Art' here referred to a distinction within *musical* practices (and art rock was a genre whose proponents were, indeed, more likely to have had music than art education) whereas our concern is with the interplay of pop and fine art ideas, much more evident now than in the art rock period. The new generation of pop culture magazines, *The Face* and *Blitz* and *i-D*, fill the shelves of the Arts Council Book Shop in Long Acre as well as the racks of provincial W.H. Smiths; they are consumer guides to the latest sounds and styles and places written in the language of art history; they embody in themselves the condition they constantly invoke – postmodernism, the collapse of high culture/low culture distinctions.

Postmodernism is a term that has been developed in a variety of different contexts – architecture, art history, literary criticism, French and German philosophies[5] – and refers, therefore, to a variety of practices and problems, but this sense of a breakdown between cultural categories is, as Jameson suggests, common to them all. The argument is that we live at a time when all cultural forms draw on the same resources, raid and make mock of each other's histories, are implicated in multi-media tie-ups (the pop video, the book of the film of the book, the image of the advertisement of the image). For most commentators the intermingling and confusion of forms means the final collapse of traditional (or, rather, in this context, modernist) cultural values, the reduction of art to the vacuous routines of mechanical production. Only among architects does there seem to be much cheerfulness about postmodernist irony and eclecticism, much confidence in the postmodern artefact.

Such a negative judgement (and we're dealing here with modernist critics of postmodern culture like Jameson rather than postmodern theorists as such, like Baudrillard) follows from the theorists' initial premise that postmodernist culture reflects a moment in the general development of capitalism rather than a progress within any particular cultural form (again architecture is a partial exception to this – postmodern buildings are explained by reference to the 'exhaustion' of modern styles). As Jameson puts it, postmodernism marks 'a new social and economic moment (or even system), which has variously been called media society, the "society of the spectacle" (Guy Debord), consumer society (or the "société de consommation"), the "bureaucratic society of controlled consumption" (Henri Lefebvre), or "postindustrial society" (Daniel Bell).'[6] Anderson is more specific:

> It was the Second World War . . . which cut off the vitality of modernism. After 1945, the old semi-aristocratic or agrarian order and its appurtenances was finished, in every country. Bourgeois democracy was finally universalised. With that, certain critical

links with a pre-capitalist past were snapped. At the same time, Fordism arrived in force. Mass production and consumption transformed the West European economies along North American lines. There could no longer be the smallest doubt as to what kind of society this technology would consolidate: an oppressively stable, monolithically industrial, capitalist civilization was now in place.[7]

The historical moment of postmodernism is also the moment of the birth of rock culture, which is, like television (and unlike film), therefore implicated in many postmodern themes: the role of the multinational communications industry; the development of technologically based leisure activities; the integration of different media forms; the significance of imagery; the fusion of art theory and sales technique. Pop songs are the soundtrack of postmodern daily life, inescapable in lifts and airports, pubs and restaurants, streets and shopping centres and sports grounds. We can't, in turn, understand the post-war history of pop without reference to the impact of Jameson's 'new kind of society', described as 'new types of consumption; planned obsolescence; an ever more rapid rhythm of fashion and styling changes; the penetration of advertising, television and the media generally; the replacement of the old tension between city and country, center and province, by the suburb and by universal standardisation; the growth of the great networks of superhighways and the arrival of automobile culture.'[8]

We'll return to this in chapter 3, but two general points follow. First, one purpose of this book is to show that critical approaches taken from fine art analysis (and resonant within postmodern theories) are more useful for making sense of popular culture than categories taken from literary criticism. The latter focus on the text when what we have to understand are the processes within which something becomes a text – processes of production and consumption.

Second, by focusing on a particular postmodern practice we want to criticize some of the assumptions of postmodern discourse itself. The recurring image used by critics is *flatness*. Dick Hebdige uses the metaphor particularly brilliantly in his tour-de-force analysis of *The Face*, 'a magazine which goes out of its way every month to blur the line between politics and parody and pastiche; the street, the stage, the screen; between purity and danger; the mainstream and the "margins": to flatten out the world.' But this is a well established image. Anderson quotes Jameson's 1971 comment: 'Henceforth, in what we may call post-industrial capitalism, the products with which we are furnished are utterly without depth: their plastic content is totally incapable of serving as a conductor of psychic energy.' And Jameson has suggested, more recently, that:

> Cultural production has been driven back inside the mind, within the monadic subject; it can no longer look directly out of its real eyes at the real world for the referent but must, as in Plato's cave, trace its mental images of the world on its confining walls. [9]

Even among the architectural writers postmodern style is defined by reference to its attention to surface details, and what's common to all these descriptions is a sense of value being ironed out. In aesthetic terms postmodern culture is essentially valueless, a fragmentary, immediate sensation which can have no grasp on experience. As Lyotard puts it:

> Eclecticism is the degree zero of contemporary general culture: one listens to reggae, watches a western, eats McDonald's food for lunch and local cuisine for dinner, wears Paris perfume in Tokyo and 'retro' clothes in Hong Kong; knowledge is a matter for TV games. It is easy to find a public for eclectic works. By becoming kitsch, art panders to the confusion which reigns in the 'taste' of the patrons. Artists, gallery owners, critics, and public wallow together in the 'anything goes', and the epoch is one of slackening. But this realism of the 'anything goes' is in fact that of money; in the absence of aesthetic criteria, it only remains possible and useful to assess the value of works of art according to the profits they yield. [10]

Even those writers who in some respects celebrate postmodernism retain this sense of contemporary life as a passing show. Marshall Berman, for example, criticizes the 'visionaries of cultural despair' for their treatment of modern life as 'uniformly hollow, sterile, flat, "one dimensional", empty of human possiblities,' but his reading of 'the signs in the street' has its own form of detachment, as if Berman were marvelling at the richness of city life precisely because it does seem to be produced by magic. The great theorists of this Marxist *flâneur* approach, Walter Benjamin and Henri Lefebvre, were, significantly, influenced by surrealism, by the suggestion of an unconscious reason, a repressed narrative at work in the play of passing images (a landscape brilliantly realized in the film *Bladerunner*). We remain, however entertained, with an image of a world beyond human control, deprived of any guiding or artistic consciousness, and while the critical task remains, in Benjamin's terms, to interpret such a reality as an illusion (not to duplicate illusion as real) the difficulties of doing so made him a melancholic (Lefebvre's spirits were revived by the Situationist International's *direct* subversion of the Spectacle in the 1960s). [11]

Flatness, once a style of painting associated with High Modernism (Barnett Newman, Mark Rothko), describes, in the postmodern art world, the collapse of all imagery into the two-dimensional message of the street hoarding. Here's a typical New York gallery story from the 1980s: 'City Arts Workshop and Adopt-a-Building sent artists to Avenue C to decorate a block-long stretch of abandoned buildings – all but one belonged to the city. People living in the neighbourhood requested that the murals depict the lively little capitalist ventures they didn't have and still don't: fake newsstand, grocery, laundromat, record store.' The city invests not in street enterprise itself, but in the illusion of street enterprise; art is no longer a critique of reality but a substitute. [12]

Put this interpretation of everyday life back into the equation of postmodern culture with the final triumph of multinational capital and you get the full-scale pessimism of contemporary art critics, whether mainstream like Robert Hughes – 'We are crammed like battery hens with stimuli, and what seems significant is not the quality or the meaning of the messages, but their excess' – or Marxist like Peter Fuller:

> We are surrounded by more visual images than appeared in any previous society in history: they comprise a torrential megavisual tradition (of which the Fine Art traditions constitute only the tiniest component) of TV, cinema, newsphotography, colour supplements, reproductions of all kinds, but, more especially, the giant bill-boards and road posters of commercial advertising. This

great stream belches down upon us everywhere we go, every minute of the day.

Sadly, this voluminous megavisual tradition attests to the unnerving health of international monopoly capitalism.[13]

This is to assume what's being asserted – the co-option of art by commerce, the superficial response of audiences, the inability of anyone (save a few, privileged critics) to grasp what is going on. But if our lives are increasingly dominated by images, by signs, then, as John A. Walker points out 'artists – being, as it were, specialists in representation – are in a unique position to call attention to these matters.'[14] Postmodern culture makes possible postmodern politics; their very involvement in the pop process gives artists new opportunities for cultural intervention. Jamie Reid, artist/designer in residence to the Sex Pistols (a sample of his graphics were bought by the Victoria and Albert Museum for £1,000 in 1980), wasn't simply advertising Pistols products in order to make money:

It was very much to create images for the street, for newspapers, for TV, which said something complicated quite simply. I mean, you could take an image like the safety-pin through the Queen or the Anarchy flag, which to me were expressing the experiences I'd had throughout the previous sixteen years. And I was coming out of the period of alternative politics, remember that.[15]

From the artist's point of view, from the pop star's, there is always a problem of audience. Who is being addressed? What for? And the answers are not irrelevant to how postmodern culture works.

Consumption and class

If one strand of postmodern culture is art-as-commodity – the aesthetic experience has changed, in Robert Hughes' words, from pseudo-religion to pseudo-possession – the other is commodity-as-art, the unfolding role in commercial production of design (a key component, as we'll see, of the history of British art education). Warren Susman notes that:

In 1934 The Museum of Modern Art (founded in 1929 and in a sense a product of the questions raised of culture in an industrial

'An image for the streets'

era) held an important show it called 'Machine Art'. Common household and industrial objects – stoves, toasters, kitchenware, chairs, vacuum cleaners, cash registers, laboratory equipment – were displayed as *works of art*.[16]

What follows from this is the merger of the visual (and avant-garde) rhetoric of art and advertising. Richard Hamilton's painting *Soft Pink Landscape*, for example, was derived from a series of colour supplement ads for Andrex toilet tissue. Later Hamilton wrote:

I was having lunch with friends in New York recently, with Bridget Riley sitting at my side. She teased me about my habitual plagiarism – even of her work. The plagiarism is self-confessed,

9

though I couldn't remember any adoption of Op ideas, except in *Epiphany* and that isn't exactly Bridget's style; I was really confused. It turned out the Andrex ads of girls in the woods that I found so inspiring were conceived by Bridget Riley when she worked at the J. Walter Thompson advertising agency. [17]

In postmodernist theory the rise of commodity aesthetics is taken to mean the collapse of 'use-value'. But even soft pink Andrex is useful, and what's really at issue here is not use-values as such but their significance to consumer choice – is Andrex any *more* useful than Bronco (or old newspaper)? Marxist theorists have long tried to distinguish between 'true' and 'false' needs to explain why people want non-subsistence goods or favour one package over another, but the suggestion now seems to be that commodities have no use-values in themselves, as material goods, at all. Our money is increasingly spent on products which are valuable only as signs relating to other signs. This marks what the influential (and opaque) French writer Jean Baudrillard calls the 'ecstasy of communication'.

Baudrillard's McLuhanesque semiotic determinism is, in effect, a new account of the high/low culture collapse, another assertion that once artistic 'autonomy' is denied by market forces then artistic experience is impossible. In becoming part of mass communication, aesthetic goods are drained of their meaning. What in high art terms is the highest form of consumption – the attribution of transcendent values to an object, the work of art – becomes within mass culture a form of madness. The consumer's purchase or possession of 'useless' goods is now just a moment of regulated exchange, its rules of meaning or, rather, conditions of meaninglessness, determined by a semiotic system beyond our control.

As Baudrillard puts it himself:

If one thinks about it, people no longer project themselves into their objects, with their affects and their representations, their fantasies of possession, loss, mourning, jealousy: the psychological dimension has in a sense vanished, and even if it can always be marked out in detail, one feels that it is not really there that things are being played out. [18]

If one thinks about it, this statement is nonsense, resting, like so much postmodern theory, on a sweeping generalization about 'people' for which there is no evidence at all. But, then, it's easy to get Baudrillard wrong. What for 'rationalist' readers seems like the description of a nightmare is, for him, the reason for celebration: people's inability to make sense of the world enables them to refuse bourgeois order. The masses 'scent the simplifying term which is behind the ideal hegemony of meaning'. Barthes and other modernist critics had suggested that mass culture is at the service of a 'regime of meaning' which could only be overthrown by the avant-garde. Baudrillard sees the masses' very passivity, their 'somnambulant strength of denial', as a gigantic black hole in which bourgeois myths are swallowed up and made truly meaningless. [19]

The Baudrillard account of atomized spectators, tribal bits in some overriding consumer circuit, ignores the historical ways in which consumption is organized, not just in terms of gender, age and class, but also along lines of taste and ideology, and once we start thinking historically the precise dating of 'postmodernism' becomes difficult. As Walter Benjamin pointed out, even by 1900 'the mass marketing of dreams within a class system that prevented their realisation in anything but symbolic form was quite obviously a growth industry'; and in her pioneering study of mass consumption in late-nineteenth-century France, Rosalind Williams reveals the origins of numerous postmodern concerns. As she points out, the development of the Parisian department store marked the arrival of a society in which what mattered was not the abundance of consumer goods as such but the ever present *vision* of such abundance (a vision which, in the twentieth century, has been embodied in images of America). Department stores were organized around displays – in windows, under counters, through packaging and advertisement – and by the end of the century such display could draw on all the magical effects of electric lighting. Visual languages have been, ever since, central to mass culture (hence our concerns in this book) but, as Williams goes on to stress, consumption was from the start a form of social (and not just semiotic) action:

> As environments of mass consumption, department stores were, and still are, places where consumers are an audience to be enter-

tained by commodities, where selling is mingled with amusement, where arousal of free-floating desire is as important as immediate purchase of particular items. Other examples of such environments are expositions, trade fairs, amusement parks, and (to cite more contemporary examples) shopping malls and large new airports or even subway stations.[20]

Mass consumption didn't dissolve class differences but gave them new forms of expression. In France, Williams suggests, the difference between bourgeois and mass consumption (which until the end of the Second World War meant middle-class rather than proletarian spending) was not that the bourgeois consumed more, but that the fantasies realized through their consumption were different – the bourgeoisie still dreamt of 'social status, respectability and security', the new mass consumers proliferated more exotic images of 'luxury and leisure'. And consumer dreams weren't just a matter of class or status expression; they were the subject too of moral and political assessment and choice. In an important passage Williams suggests that:

> With the aid of ideal types two distinct consumer styles may be seen emerging in the 1880s and the 1890s: an elitist type and a democratic one. For all their differences in detail, many, if not most, of the experiments in consumer models of those decades fall into one or the other of these categories. Both the elitist and the democratic consumers rebelled against the shortcomings of mass and bourgeois styles of consumption, but in seeking an alternative they moved in opposite directions. Elitist consumers considered themselves a new type of aristocracy, one not of birth but of spirit – superior individuals who would forge a personal mode of consumption far above the banalities of the everyday. Democratic consumers sought to make consumption more equal and participatory. They wanted to rescue everyday consumption from banality by raising it to the level of a political and social statement.[21]

What is fascinating about this is that in describing two modes of consumption Williams is describing two different *artistic* responses to the problem of creativity in the mass market place. These responses are central to the history of British art education in which we can see, quite clearly, the 'democratic' influence of the arts and craft movement on the one hand, the 'elitist' influence of bohemia on the other. Indeed, one of our concerns here is to trace these art school movements back into pop consumption – Williams' Parisian dandies, for example, would be at home immediately among the poseurs in the *Face* or the new pop stars on *The Tube*, while her democrats now sit behind Red Wedge's trestle tables.

The point is that the aestheticization of commodities, the association of consumption with fantasy and dream, doesn't make it thoughtless (any more than high art is thoughtless) or valueless (any more than high art is valueless). To choose Andrex over Bronco on the basis of its packaging does mean making some sort of judgement – and it's how that judgement works that the designers and packagers and advertisers themselves spend so much time and money trying to understand.

If the industry is now dominated, in Rachel Bowlby's words, 'by selling techniques involving the making of beautiful images', and consumer choices now rest on responses to those images, on the assignment of qualities like grace and beauty to toilet tissue rather than to paintings, then the rise of mass consumption has made possible a new profession of skilled image makers, specialists, to quote Richard Hamilton, 'in the look of things'. The question this raises (and it is central to the organization of art schools) is the relationship between the traditional fine artist and the contemporary commercial artist. The conventional distinction is well expressed by Roy McMullen in his survey of twentieth-century arts for the *Encyclopaedia Britannica* in 1968. 'Popular art', to use his term,

> is created (in many instances 'calculated' would be a more accurate term) by artists who differ from the serious, or elite, artists in their tendency to express not their own views of life, but rather the views they think the customer has. Consequently popular art is often scarcely art at all; it is often literally meretricious. It makes use of artistic means for non-artistic ends. [22]

More generally, McMullen distinguishes the 'free' pursuit of the fine arts from 'unfree' applied arts like design and decoration, 'tied to domestic, commercial, technological and other nonaesthetic considerations'. But this distinction is hard to maintain when commercial considerations *are* aesthetic considerations. Richard Hamilton, in his controversial 1959 discussion of the 'new professional class whose task is to fashion the appearance of objects in everyday use' had already suggested that 'goods that sell to consumers must show the hand of the stylist'. His point was that there isn't a fixed consumer taste to which every new product must conform:

> The mass arts, or pop arts, are not popular arts in the old sense of art arising from the masses. They stem from a professional group with a highly developed cultural sensibility. As in any art, the most valued products will be those which emerge from a strong personal conviction and these are often the products which succeed in a competitive market. [23]

Subsequent art critics have been unimpressed by Hamilton's celebration of the stylist. As Adrian Forty puts it, there remains a 'crucial distinction' between art and design – 'art objects are usually both conceived and made by (or under the direction of) one person, the artist, whereas this is not so with manufactured goods . . . calling industrial design "art" suggests that designers occupy the principal role in production, a misconception which effectively severs most of the connections between design and the processes of society.' But it was the processes of society which most interested Hamilton too. As he suggested, the problem of commercial art is not how to subject the artist to the consumer but how to subject the consumer to the artist:

> It will take longer to breed desire for possession when the objects to be possessed have sprung not directly from the subconscious of the consumer but from the creative consciousness of an artistic sensibility – but the time-lag will have distinct advantages for industry . . . [it] . . . can be used to design a consumer to the product and (s)he can be 'manufactured' during the production span. Then producers should not feel inhibited, need not be disturbed by doubts about the reception their products may have by an audience they do not trust, the consumer can come from the same drawing board. [24]

A point Marx made, more abstractly, a century ago:

14

An objet d'art creates a public that has artistic taste and is able to enjoy beauty – and the same can be said of any other product. Production accordingly produces not only an object for the subject, but also a subject for the object. [25]

Hamilton's (and Marx's) 'shocking' suggestion that consumers can be 'produced' is one of the operational rules of pop music. As Dave Laing writes, 'musicians are involved at the stage which in other industries would be called design: the preparation of a prototype from which mass production can begin', and the biggest and most influential stars (David Bowie is the most obvious example) are precisely the ones who design their own *fans* – this is one source of the tension between art school-influenced pop musicians and industry assumptions about 'giving the public what they want'. [26]

What's startling about Hamilton's position then, is not that he was wrong, but that he seemed to accept consumer manipulation with such equanimity. What's under threat here is the autonomy – or perhaps the authority – of consumers: their 'free' choice is not 'really' theirs. Hamilton himself put this into perspective in a speech to the National Union of Teachers' conference on 'Popular Culture and Personal Responsibility' in 1960 (an occasion where many of the basic British lines on 1960s mass culture were first spelt out):

In 1949 I went to the cinema about three times a week, a compulsion which had little to do with the merits of the films I saw; Rank cinemas, at that time, showed a healthy profit. In the late fifties, as my attendance at the cinema declined, I became aware that my thoughtless change of habit had created a crisis in the film industry, not only was Rank losing money but I had even caused severe cuts in production at major Hollywood studios. A few weeks after I purchased a camera I read of the fantastic increase in sales of amateur photographic equipment. If I buy paperbacks instead of cloth-bound books the publishing industry makes a fuss about paperbacks taking over. When I bought just one car we had a national traffic problem . . . [27]

The point Hamilton is making is that most of our 'individual' decisions reflect, in fact, collective social forces and this is as true of our aesthetic tastes as anything else. For most cultural commentators

15

(who write as if they're quite free of such social forces) the individual's subordination to collective tastes and, in particular, to collective changes of taste, is a measure of effective commercial manipulation. But, as Hamilton says (and as dedicated followers of pop fashion we'd emphasize) it doesn't *feel* like that. There obviously is manipulation, but consumers are quite used to spotting and resisting it; at issue here are not just 'mindless' fantasies or unconscious desires but also self-conscious decisions and choices. And these need to be understood (not dismissed) just as much by people opposing the power of consumer capitalism as by the capitalist sales force itself.

Subjectivity

For critics of postmodern culture the central deceit of mass consumption is that the sales stress on individual 'free' choice in the market place – consumption as self-expression – is made in the pursuit of uniformity: consumption as a way of being like everyone else. In practice, though, what's involved is a play of identity and difference of which this simpleminded distinction makes no sense. We become who we are – in terms of taste and style and political interest and sexual preference – through a whole series of responses to people and images, identifying with some, distinguishing ourselves from others, and through the interplay of these decisions with our material circumstances (as blacks or whites, males or females, workers or non-workers). Advertisers intervene *within* these processes, relating lives to lifestyles, to the accumulation of purchases.

In her study of the origins of French mass consumption, Williams suggests that what matters here is not the desire for the commodity itself but for the way of life which, advertisers suggest, can be reached *via* the commodity – which is why, in Baudrillard's terms, its value is as a sign. Our argument is that while advertisers use this fantasy system, they don't exhaust it. People's sense of themselves has always come from the use of images and symbols (signs of nation, class and sexuality, for example). How else do politics and religion, and art itself, work? Indeed, one argument made by radical pop musicians (as we'll describe in chapter 4) is that the blatancy of advertisers' attempts to create such images is what allows us to break out of social conditioning, to make ourselves up just like our 'models' on the screen or record player.

What's most important about mass culture is not the drive towards standardization, but the constant call on consumers to achieve the impossible: 'Be yourself!' The American historian Warren Susman comments that if 'one of the things that makes the modern world "modern" is the development of consciousness of self', it is also true that what is meant by 'self' shifts as the social structure and its tensions change. The early capitalist/protestant emphasis on 'character' – a self moulded by discipline – has given way in the twentieth century to the self as 'personality', the unique expression of each individual's own, personal qualities. But, as Susman shows, in the resulting flood of American guides to 'self-improvement' the recurring statement is that 'Personality is the quality of being Somebody' – standing out from the crowd. In Susman's words, 'the social role demanded of all in the new culture of personality was that of a performer.'[28]

Our sense of self, in short, comes from our *public* presence; what makes consumer goods desirable is, precisely, that they make possible the public display of 'private' qualities. In this consumer world the stars – film stars in the 1930s, pop stars today – are the 'experts' from whom we learn our performing techniques. It is in this management of our 'public' and 'private' selves that the real power of commodities is revealed: they produce us as *sexed* subjects, define masculinity and femininity, code them along lines of possession and desire.

From the start of industrial capitalism, personal – 'domestic' – consumption was associated with women, and women's consumption was associated with style. As a succession of cotton print masters explained to the 1840 Select Committee on the Copyright of Designs, it was the variety (rather than quality) of their patterns which was profitable. Did more patterns mean more dresses bought and worn?

> I think it is exceedingly probable, because what is a dress after all? It is mere fancy and taste, it is not a mere covering, otherwise we should not have had any printed dresses at all. It is like paintings, there is no reason why a gentleman should possess a painting, but when he sees a good one, he wishes to have it.[29]

17

The gender division here is familiar – the female concern for dress is 'mere fancy', gentlemen are interested in paintings – but this manufacturer was still philistine enough to equate fashion and art. Nineteenth-century aesthetic theorists became increasingly concerned to distinguish the two – to defend art against commerce – while retaining the gendered terms. The implicit contrast of serious (male) creation and silly (female) fancy remains central to the mass culture debate. However important women's expenditure to the rise of the mass market, the decisions on which it rests are dismissed as trivial, the results simply of market manipulation. In her study of 'proto-industrialization', Maxine Berg notes that: 'Eighteenth-century moralists singled out girls and women in their attacks on luxury expenditure, complaining of girls buying silk ribbons, hats, jewellery and dresses to suit every change in fashion.'[30]

Men, in fact, 'equally participated in the luxury consumption of dress' – Berg cites the skilled calico printers of Bury, who 'displayed themselves at festivals in breeches, white silk stockings, silver buckles and powdered hair' – but already such a care for clothes seemed 'effeminate'. Fashionable males (beaux and dandies, screen idols and pop stars) always offend moralists, always suggest an unmanly concern for selfish pleasures over public duties, and postmodern critics have mostly gone along with this judgement and its implicit gender terms – the rise of fashion and frippery measures the trivialization of art.

In fact, as Elizabeth Wilson argues,

> Fashion is a branch of aesthetics, of the art of modern society. It is also a mass pastime, a form of group entertainment, of popular culture. Related as it is to both fine art and popular art, it is a kind of performance art.[31]

And fashion can't be disentangled from pop music. The history of rock, in Britain at least, is a history of image as well as sound, a history of cults and cultures defined by clothes as well as songs. Whether in pursuit of authenticity or artifice, romantic truth or postmodern paradox and pastiche, musicians use the language of fashion, and this may be the point at which art schools have their most important musical impact – in college terms, fashion courses stand formally for what the would-be music-makers are exploring informally: the interplay of aesthetic and commercial judgement, the equation of personal expression with mass taste. And sex and gender are irrevocably implicated in these matters – even in straight empirical terms, fashion design tends to be a 'female' subject in art schools; most of the would-be pop stars are male.

A final point on gender and art, consumption and bohemia. Just as fashion, the sign of women's visual taste, has never been taken seriously by aestheticians, so women's central consuming activity, shopping, has never been taken seriously by sociologists. Men idling through the city, ogling passers-by, hanging about on street corners, absorbed in city spectacle, adding to city noise, have long been romanticized in the language of gang and subculture, were dignified even in the nineteenth century by the term *flâneur* (rather than the less flattering *voyeur*). Women on the streets are simply seen as going about their business. 'Although consumerism is a central aspect of modernity,' writes Janet Wolff in her examination of the literature of modernism, 'the peculiar characteristics of "the modern" – the fleeting, anonymous encounter and the purposeless strolling – do not apply to shopping.' But this literary judgement – gazing out of café windows given the weight of melancholia, gazing into shop windows dismissed as time-wasting – misses the way in which shopping, particularly for young women, is, indeed, an idle aesthetic experience, an opportunity for nostalgia, daydream and desire. The point is not that men and women have different experiences of the city, but, rather, that the experiences they share – strolling, shopping, drinking, chatting – are defined along gender lines. Rachel Bowlby suggests that the rise of the consumer society meant, in late nineteenth-century practice, a masculine appeal to women to buy: 'the making of willing consumers readily fitted into the available ideological paradigm of a seduction of women by men, in which women would be addressed as yielding objects to the powerful male subject forming, and informing them of, their desires.'[32]

The 'passivity' of consumers is thus derived from an assumption about their femininity (an analogy still used by Baudrillard). In pop terms this means the appeal of young male stars to even younger female fans, a relationship which has always troubled self-conscious pop 'artists', but the truth is that the male/female organization of consumer culture is much more complicated than the imagery of passive consumption implies – gender ideologies are cut across by patterns of desire which can't so easily be sexed. Read their fantasies and 'passive' fans turn out to be erotically active and highly sociable; if they feel strangely possessed *by* their idols, they take their revenge in the imaginary possession *of* them. Sexuality is a matter of imagination for all concerned, the point where to consume (and to be consumed) seems to confirm us most vividly as individuals.[33]

Mass consumption has an equally significant role in the formation of collective identity: here too the images are put into play among numerous other signs and symbols of collectivity. In August 1976 the artist and film-maker Derek Jarman wrote a sour note in his diary about the 'gang of King's Road fashion anarchists who call themselves punks'.

> The music business has conspired with them to create another working-class myth as the dole queues grow longer to fuel the flames. But in reality the instigators of punk are the same old petit-bourgeois art students, who a few months ago were David Bowie and Bryan Ferry look-alikes – who've read a little art history and adopted Dadaist typography and bad manners, and are now in the business of reproducing a fake street credibility. No-one will admit that in a generation brought up on the consensus values of TV there is no longer such a thing as working-class 'culture'.[34]

What Jarman seems to mean by this is that there is no longer a working-class culture springing directly from some essential working-class experience. It's doubtful that there ever was. Working-class culture has always been the result of the interaction of experience and myth and what Jarman is really decrying is the new source of myths – the music business, TV and petit-bourgeois art students! Jarman's tone of voice – bitter, weary, vaguely left-wing – is, in fact, common among the very musicians he's criticizing, and is, indeed, another aspect of postmodernism – the collapse of the political certainty of radicals since Marxism or, rather, the proletariat lost its authority as the voice of the future. Nineteenth-century Romantic artists were anti-industrial and found truth in nature, twentieth-century Romantic socialists were anti-capitalist and found truth in the working class, but all the New Romantics can do is celebrate consumption and find truth in the fleeting, flashing signs of the metropolis. It's as if artists, conscious of their own artifice, still crave for some unambiguous mark of authenticity and are thus haunted by the idea of *real* street credibility. If consumers seek to transcend the everyday – to be truly themselves – through fantasies of the extraordinary, there's a significant strand of bohemian thought that romanticizes normality. Pop music takes its power from the consequent meeting of consumer fantasies of difference and musicians' fantasies of collectivity.

Low theory

As should be clear by now, the apparently narrow issue of the relation of rock and art schools is, in fact, a useful way to focus the much broader problems of the relationships of art and commerce, high and low culture, what we've been describing as the postmodern condition. There is one last point to make about this. Our discussions will, inevitably, refer to the most sophisticated pop theorists from within the worlds of art and music. What relevance do their accounts of what they do have for 'ordinary' consumers? In answering this it's important to remember the theories of pop

> developed out of day-to-day practices of pop itself, out of people's need to bring some sort of order and justification to the continuing processes of musical evaluation, choice and commitment – whether such people are musicians, entrepreneurs or fans. The practice of pop involves, in short, the practice of theorising. Perhaps we should call the results low theory – confused, inconsistent, full of hyperbole and silence, but still theory, and theory which is compelled by necessity to draw key terms and assumptions from high theory, from the more systematic accounts of art, commerce, pleasure and class that are available.[35]

Aesthetic theories, as Peter Bürger puts it, are no longer 'the exclusive domain of philosophers'. There are numerous mediating institutions between theories of art and everyday exercises of taste – the artists themselves, a variety of educational settings, critics, publicists, etc. 'Everyone,' wrote Gramsci, 'finally, outside his or her professional activity, carries on some form of intellectual activity, that is, is a "philosopher", an artist, possesses taste, participates in a particular conception of the world.'[36] What we want to suggest is that in the history of rock this conception of the world has been derived from issues and arguments originating in the particular problems of culture and commerce posed by art education. The resulting play of high and low theory is sometimes obvious, as in this comment from Paul Morley in *Blitz*:

> As Frankie Goes to Hollywood became tabloid stuff, the toilet papers were talking to me, the *Mail*, the *News of the World*, the *Express*, delighting me with their rotten misquotes, and some journals even began quoting McLuhan and McLaren in connection with my involvement – a further delight, if only because it is *obvious* that Roland Barthes, Saatchi and Saatchi and Jonathan King are more relevant.[37]

And sometimes indirect, as in the recurring importance of art schools simply as a *scene*, a place where young people, whether students there or not, can hang out and learn/fantasize what it means to be an artist, a bohemian, a star – this is the art school dance that goes on forever.

What cuts across art training and consumption is the need to be 'a bit different' (the reason given by one young Coventry woman for hanging around the Poly's art school discos), and for more than thirty years now art school students have been the youth group who've articulated most clearly and influentially what 'difference' can mean. Most pop musicians, of course, haven't been to art schools. They come into the profession from school groups, music training, the traditional local routes of semi-pro club and pub appearance, each of which backgrounds provides its own account of what good pop music is and how it works. But they too want to be different – if only as stars – and so art school ideology interrelates with their 'professional' ideas as well as with those of the music business itself. If there are, then, occasionally, performing scenes in which art ideas are obviously dominant (the Mercer Arts Center in New York in the early 1970s, St Martin's in the late 1970s, Liverpool, maybe, in the early 1960s), in day-to-day pop terms, they swirl about with many others. That they are there anyway is what we hope to show.

22

Conclusion

In researching this book we've been continually surprised by how little interest art writers take in music. Pop critics take the art school connection for granted (even if they say little interesting about it); art critics, with the exception of John A. Walker, seem to ignore the music connection altogether. What this reflects is the continued importance of traditional notions of creative authority: pop stars, it seems, are simply not recognizable as 'artists'. Even in postmodernist

'Roland Barthes, Saatchi & Saatchi, Jonathan King'

discussions of new high art uses of pop cultural forms (and vice versa) Laurie Anderson is hailed as the *only* crossover act. For Walker, 'Anderson's success indicates that the barrier between the realms of fine art and mass culture is not absolute. But this is an exceptional case.' For Hal Foster, she is equally exceptional, a postmodernist who 'uses the art-historical or pop cultural cliché against itself, in order to decenter the (masculine) subject of such representation, to pluralize the social self, to render cultural meanings ambiguous, indeterminate.'[38]Anderson works for such writers in the way Bruce Springsteen does for champions of rock's blue-collar 'truth' – she's the star necessary to validate the theory. The point, though, is not to find the authentic artist amidst the pop cultural dross but to see what happens to art ideas as they are diffused in pop generally.

The only other place they seem to be recognizable to cultural critics is in pop videos, which have already generated more high theoretical words than pop music itself – even Walker asserts that promo videos 'are presently the vehicles for the most creative ideas being expressed in the mass media'. This seems an odd conclusion – from a pop fan's point of view videos represent the imposition of some rather tired clichés (from the history of cinema, advertising and pornography) onto the music. As Brian Eno put it: 'most video art is like someone describing, not very well, a film they saw.'[39] Again it seems that art critics need conventional 'visuals' to recognize something as art, even though the history of pop stars' live (and still) performing images contains pictures just as imaginative (and artistic) as in the average pop video.

Both these examples indicate the continued power in art criticism of the argument that mass media exclude real creativity. The assumption is that technology/capital logic shapes mass culture which, in turn, provides people with particular sorts of ideological experience; there is no moment in this chain when artists have the power to do anything but occasionally (Laurie Anderson) reveal contradictions. Our assumption, by contrast, is that people embedded in particular ideologies and experiences shape communication technologies and thus shape mass culture. This is not to deny the power of capital but to assert that, nevertheless, cultural producers can and do make significant decisions, can and do draw on ideas of what it is to be an artist. The best pop musicians respond to the ideological problems of their place in a commercial process and so make music that resonates for their listeners. If nothing else, then, we want to bring politics back into discussion of postmodern culture. Our position is that British pop music is made through struggles and arguments that can only be understood by references to art school connections. As Andreas Huyssen has written, the only point of adopting the term postmodernism is because 'it operates in a field of tension between tradition and innovation, conservation and renewal, mass culture and high art in which the second terms are no longer automatically privileged over the first.'[40] We need to rethink cultural politics by re-examining cultural practice.

In one of the purpler passages in his study of modernity, Marshall Berman writes:

> To be modern is to experience personal and social life as a mael-strom, to find one's world and oneself in perpetual disintegration and renewal, trouble and anguish, ambiguity and contradiction: to be part of a universe in which all that is solid melts into air. To be a modern*ist* is to make oneself somehow at home in the maelstrom, to make its rhythms one's own, to move within its currents in search of the forms of reality, of beauty, of freedom, of justice, that its fervid and perilous flow allows.[41]

In London at the start of the 1960s, to be a modernist meant 'total devotion to looking and being "cool". Spending practically all your money on clothes and all your after work hours in clubs and dance halls.' This observer, Richard Barnes, 'wasn't a Mod and never even thought of being a Mod. I was at Art School. My involvement with Mods came because my friend from Art School, with whom I shared a flat, played in a group . . .'[42]

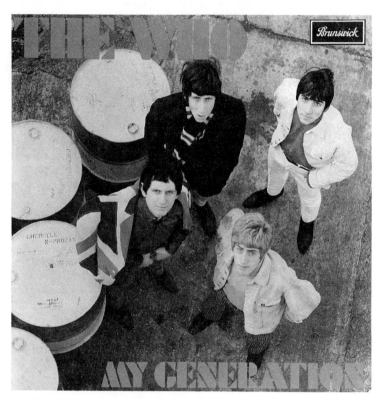

Modernists

2
THE ART SCHOOL CONTEXT

Many people (mainly Americans) fail to understand why so many rock musicians have art school backgrounds. The simple fact is that if you have any artistic talent, you can groove along on a grant, go to a few lectures, enjoy an excellent social life, rehearse in any spare rooms, meet similarly inclined students, get posters done for nothing, prepare for stardom!

(Pete Frame)[1]

Every fucking art student that plays out of tune gets a record deal.

(Willy DeVille)[2]

The art school is unique in British higher education. It condones and encourages an attitude of learning through trial and error, through day-to-day experiment rather than through instruction. Bauhaus's Kevin Haskins recalls his first day at Northampton Art School:

It was mind opening. I hadn't been in contact with people like that before. If you can imagine this on your first day after leaving school, they took us into this hall where there were 12-inch squares mapped out on the floor and ceiling and pieces of string hanging down to make each one like a small cage. They told us to create our own environments within those squares and gave us all day to do it.[3]

Traditionally, certainly during the 1950s and early 1960s, art schools' loose entry requirements – welcoming the talented but academically relatively unqualified, searching for the oblique answer at selection interviews – set them apart from the staid universities and more rigorous professional and craft training colleges, even though the National Diploma in Design had fairly formal syllabus and exam procedures. Art as knowledge, art as a vocation, carries unusual inflections.

Alexei Sayle taught drama and Ivor Cutler poetry at Chelsea in the late 1970s. Ian Dury, recalling his art teaching career, said 'Actually I didn't know that much about art myself . . . I mean, I knew who Van Gogh was, but mostly I just bluffed it. . . . Mostly I just let 'em get on with it.' Art schools, understanding irony, tolerate virtues of fun and play rather than imposing a rigid work ethic; indeed a tolerance of students who work with complete self-indulgence is common. One ex-art student, a contemporary of Sade's at Colchester, told us that, faced with the career choice of a foundation course or journalism training, he chose art because it was 'the most risky occupation I could think of '.[4] The unsettling question amongst students is 'what is it about me, what do they like, why do they want me?' They're seldom told.

But contrary to popular stereotypes, most art students do work hard. In learning conditions other undergraduates would find adverse, even frightening, art school students commonly work eight-hour days, often into the night. The art school experience is about commitment to a working practice, to a mode of learning which assumes the status of lifestyle. Art school students are recruited into a meritocracy which sets itself apart from the usual rules of wealth and class. In the words of one of them, 'art and design education does not reflect social privilege in the most straightforward way. It is not infiltrated by the public schools, nor infested with parental income.'[5] College entry often changes outlook profoundly – attitudes to art, clothes, friendships dissolve and reform. The first year, particularly with fine art courses, is given to forgetting previous training and experience (like most of us, young art students get their basic knowledge of art from television and the Sunday supplements; their grasp of art movements is vague and rhetorical). But the process of amnesia runs deeper, into cultural attitudes and behaviour. Other students discover drinking, drugs, a freedom of sexual relationships alongside tutorials and library visits; art school students discover a new identity. One would be unlikely to overhear an engineering or accountancy (or even sociology or literature) student expressing the same sentiments about their discipline: 'Art is everything. Art is life.'

Like other students, artists frequently challenge their training – its relevance, their teachers' ability – but they add profound doubts about whether their practice is teachable in the first place. One Camberwell painting student, asked whether she believed art college training was necessary to understand art, replied:

> It's about trying to get into the world of art . . . a chance to meet other people who paint, as opposed to getting a degree. The tutors are just people who are interested in painting – some of the students are better than the tutors at talking about it. [6]

Unlike most undergraduates, art school students leave college fully trained; unlike, say, engineering, architecture, law and medical students, they don't need postgraduate courses or formal work experience to fit them for practice. On the other hand, postgraduate study at a prestigious college – the RCA or the Slade, say – is regarded as necessary for a fulltime fine art career, a reflection of the fact that art education forms the most extensive and accessible system of artistic patronage in Britain. Since nearly all practising artists do some teaching it can be argued that in Britain the art schools *are* the art world. It certainly remains all but impossible to gain status (and market value) as a painter or sculptor completely outside them.

Even today, after two decades of pruning and rationalization, there are still more art schools in Britain per head of population than anywhere else. And British art schools are unlike others. [7] All art schools carry and nurture attitudes to work and leisure, style and life: in Britain this ideological stress has been conditioned by 150 years of argument about art and design's cultural use and function. The modern British art school has evolved through a repeated series of attempts to gear its practice to trade and industry to which the schools themselves have responded with a dogged insistence on spontaneity, on artistic autonomy, on the need for independence, on the power of the arbitrary gesture. Art as free practice versus art as a response to external demand: the state and the art market define the problem; the art school modernizes, individualizes, adds nuances to the solution. The references and sources change, but what remains important is the idea of artistic *practice*, art as a specific kind of labour.

The art school emphasis on creativity and artistic distance has bred a peculiar attitude to commercial success. Art school students are marginal, in class terms, because art, particularly fine art, is marginal in cultural terms. Constant attempts to reduce the marginality of art education, to make art and design more 'responsive' and 'vocational' by gearing them towards industry and commerce, have confronted the ideology of 'being an artist', the Romantic vision which is deeply embedded in the art school experience. Even as pop stars, art students celebrate the critical edge marginality allows, turning it into a sales technique, a source of celebrity.

Being an artist

We must realise also in looking at Jameson's notion of the 'subject' as a monad-like character how deeply specific parts of the Romantic aspiration have penetrated modern art school teaching and helped form the paradigm of the expressive self so beloved of art school milieu. (Terry Atkinson)[8]

Early experiments in art education contrast vividly with the above picture of the contemporary art school experience. The first modern British art and design school, later to become the Royal College of Art, developed out of industry's concern at the poor standard of British finished goods compared to European competition.[9] The argument was about the absence of professional design education. The 1836 Report of the Select Committee on Arts and Manufactures – to which the first government school of design was a response the following year – succinctly stated:

This scanty supply of instruction is the more to be lamented because it appears that there exists among the enterprising and laborious classes of our country an earnest desire for information in the Arts.[10]

Organized around William Dyce's philosophy that there was a positive science of design and that creativity was an irrelevant diversion, the Schools of Design system cemented the division between fine art and commercial art that still underpins the art school network and informs higher educational planning. [11]

There was a double-edged problem for early administrators trying to establish the importance of art and design education for industry. On the one hand, there was the suspicion, aired in 1836 and still circulating widely today in DES and college circles, that British industry was neither interested in nor understood the concept of good design in the first place. On the other hand, the reformers had to confront a solidifying artistic ideology and practice which refused to be constrained by industrial demands. Initially teaching was dour and pragmatic, the classrooms sombre and severe, but as the schools of design spread nationally they increasingly adopted fine art identities and by the 1850s had absorbed the Romantic assertion that art had something unsettling to say about industrial culture, was not meant to reinforce its limitations.

Romanticism reflected the artist's sense of cultural displacement under capitalism, the changed material location of artistic practice. The eighteenth century had seen the decline of direct patronage and commission, the emergence of the 'free' artist and craftsman no longer bound to depict and celebrate aristocratic wealth, but dependent instead on the uncertainties of the emerging capitalist market. As Ernst Fischer puts it: 'Previously the artisan had worked to order to a particular client. The commodity producer in the capitalist world now worked for an unknown buyer.' [12]

In the seventeenth century work not directly commissioned had been sold in street markets, but these couldn't meet the aspirations of free artists, and what emerged and solidified over the next century was a more sophisticated system of sale and exchange, with dealer networks – painting shops – replacing the primacy of temporary shows like the Royal Academy's annual exhibition. What emerged too was a system of criticism and publicity (first through galleries and museums, then, additionally, through journals). Taken together, this represented a new organizational base for artistic practice, forming the modern system of market patronage, a network of institutions governing general access to and knowledge about art.

Romanticism, as a continuing ideology of free artistic practice, was fine art's response to these institutions, external to its practice, but mediating between art and society, between artist and buyer and audience. Artists, in other words, continued to take the notion of freedom seriously; to believe, following Schiller, that only art could transcend social profanity and produce moral and aesthetic perfection. They countered calls for responsibility with the rhetoric of autonomy – it was their 'independence' that guaranteed artists' cultural value, the superiority of their vision. The irony of this position (an irony which was to have significant practical consequences for twentieth-century art schools) was that the Romantic critique of industrial capitalism became the source of the bourgeoisie's own evaluation of art. In Peter Bürger's words:

> The *autonomy of art* is a category of bourgeois society. It permits the description of art's detachment from the context of practical life as a historical development – that among the members of those classes which, at least at times, are free from the pressures of the need for survival, a sensuousness could evolve that was not part of any means-end relationships. Here we find the moment of truth in the talk about the autonomous work of art. What this category cannot lay hold of is that this detachment of art from practical contexts is a *historical process*, i.e. that it is socially conditioned. And here lies the untruth of the category.... The relative dissociation of the work of art from the praxis of life in bourgeois society thus becomes transformed into the (erroneous) idea that the work of art is totally independent of society. [13]

But while this has meant that individual artists have been able to justify their 'uselessness' by reference to the 'higher' values of creativity, it hasn't prevented their day-to-day experience of embattlement. This is as obvious in the ideology of modernity as in the idea of autonomy. If the new artistic personality took capitalist modernity seriously, adopting the slogan of constant change and innovation, the power of the new over the traditional and the old, then this obsessive striving for a new art, for a new language of aesthetic communication, had its material roots in Romanticism's attempt to make sense of a fluid capitalist culture's demands. But, at the same time, there seemed to be a natural personal antagonism between the bourgeoisie (stolid, respectable) and the modern artist (scruffy and vain) – their lives were organized around differing definitions of work and play. The modern artist became the 'outsider', serving no immediate function the capitalist class could understand, except as a kind of harbinger of change – as artist Donald Judd recently observed, 'it's to the credit of artists that for them dying institutions invalidate themselves earlier than for others.'[14]

In personal terms to live Romanticism meant taking on what we will call bohemianism – a way of life in which autonomy is indicated by unconventionality, the private 'escape' from market relations is a matter of public gesture, Art for Art's Sake is pitched against social responsibility. The relocation of art within capitalist culture became, in short, the material basis for art as lifestyle – a style dependent on the tension between a private world of creative autonomy and the public demands of the art market.

But perhaps the most significant intrusion into the tranquillity of individual creation has been art education – partly an attempt to professionalize (make respectable) artistic practice, more threateningly, an attempt to make it, and its practitioners, more useful. The Schools of Design were intended for artisans not artists, but even they were well-versed in the creative stance. Romanticism, in all its political and stylistic shades, gripped the nineteenth-century artist's imagination: art education became the natural setting for the bohemian battle with convention. The Schools of Design's pragmatic, slavish system was rapidly challenged by their students' counter commitment to pure aestheticism; the schools became, despite themselves, Schools of Art.[15]

This development was encouraged by their staff, equally sympathetic to fine art ideas, but the most damning attacks on the state system came from Romantic idealists with no immediate occupational axes to grind. John Ruskin, for example, condemned the art educators' specific attempts to give the students 'such accurate command to mathematical form as may afterwards enable them to design rapidly and cheaply for manufactures,' as well as the wider purpose of suiting art to commerce.[16] In the pursuit of art's truth to nature, Ruskin looked into history; echoing Schlegel and the German Romantics, he found a fusion of intellectual and manual labour as the model for artistic training – a fusion lost by the machine age and capitalist rationality. Ruskin's work in the Pre-Raphaelite educational experiment at the London Working Men's College was an attempt to realize this counter-philosophy, to put aesthetics at the heart of art education. [17]

William Morris combined Ruskin's aesthetic position with a reading of Marx's political and economic theory and declared a 'Crusade and Holy Warfare against the Age'. Rejecting the educational split between pure art and applied design, Morris and the Arts and Crafts movement tried to fuse the two. His fundamental principle was that art is tied to everyday life; it must be both decorative and functional – Arts and Crafts took art out of the studio and the gallery and into the living room and the street. From the flowing elegance of the Pre-Raphaelite gothic revival to Wilde's barbed high camp, the second half of the nineteenth century saw the perfection of the idea of the artist as dandy, the total artistic personality. Artists like Rossetti asserted their lifestyle from the wrought iron balconies of Cheyne Walk. For a brief moment at the turn of the century art and craft were united, democratic and elitist consumers shared tastes.

The first art school to be directly influenced by Morris's ideas was Birmingham, which in 1890 added a training school for jewellers and silversmiths. The movement's major institutional successes, though, were confined to the Central School of Arts and Crafts, founded by the London County Council in 1896, and the considerable influence exercised on the formation of the Bauhaus; and, in general, advocates of Arts and Crafts or Bauhaus-style collectivity have found the British art school stress on a superior Romantic individualism difficult to penetrate. As Glyn Probert suggests:

> Art education is based upon notions of individualism and genius, which culminate, at art college, in predominantly middle-class students and tutors/working artists often rigidly adhering to these bourgeois values. Group activity is frowned upon, formal concerns are paramount, with emphasis on spontaneity and allowing the paint to 'speak'. [18]

The problem Morris faced, like the industrial pragmatists before him and the cultural studies theorists to come, is that artists *believe* in the mystery of individual creation. Take this quote from Roger Hilton:

> At the Frontiers of what had been done and what is
> about to be done stands the creative artist. The
> unknown facing him like an abyssal orifice.
> He must jump!
> Freedom?
> That he had.
> But such freedom as not many can stand. [19]

Hilton is emphasizing the existential quality of painting *practice.*
Creating a way of seeing means creating a way of life. Van Gogh and
Gauguin project the popular image of this – the inner struggle, the
escape, the passionate gesture – but, less dramatically, Hilton and the
St Ives group of 'primitive' Romantics demonstrated the idiosyncratic flights of the British tradition. They escaped to Cornwall
because it was far removed from the market.

Romantic idealism conditions artistic behaviour and lifestyle in
more subtle ways too, through the constant striving to create new
work, through the thrust to modernize. The point is made by painter
Adrian Berg:

> Tradition for an artist doesn't mean what he should do but what
> he is up against. What one has to do . . . is to make up one's own
> tradition. One then finds one's own way vis-à-vis this. The
> mistake many artists make is to think they can do what they like.
> They end up doing what someone else has already done. If they
> had a tradition to work against they'd be unable to come up with
> something so pat. [20]

Perhaps the loss of a tradition, even to rebel against, marks the
change from modernity to postmodernity, but the real significance
of Berg's comments is that they suggest the importance of the art
school to Romantic ideology. Art schools place constant emphasis
on experimental practice, but also preserve art's traditions, teach the
established art techniques against which students are expected to
rebel. Art school students have usually accepted the challenge,
showing a healthy disdain for the demands of the past – except, that
is, for the Romantic demand that being an artist means living as an
artist. In art school rhetoric, this means that art is held to dissolve the
capitalist work/leisure distinction. Or, in the words of a Hornsey

student in 1968, 'I believe that this hope to work for one's living by living in one's work is a reason why many of us choose to go to art school.' Even then (let alone by the 1980s) art school experience was an anachronism, with students desperately clinging on to attitudes to work and play which had otherwise vanished.

The art school experience is about freedom and experimentation, doing what you like and not really caring whether anyone else likes it, puzzling outsiders and infuriating rate-payers, creating 'your own structure', at your own pace and in your own style. Art school students are unlike other students because art schools are unlike other colleges. They play on sensibilities and cultivate talents which present an opaque screen to the uninitiated. Perhaps the most telling comment comes from Richard Hamilton:

> The art schools should be seen as places where civilised behaviour can be taught better than anywhere else. As more people become unemployed, the more of them that become artists the better. As soon as students finish their course, the government should put them on a pension. [21]

The civilizing properties of art schools are, though, differently arranged between course specializations, with the most glaring and growing disparities – of temperament and career aspiration, practice and ideology – between fine art and graphic design students.

The Design Council's comprehensive handbook, *Design Courses in Britain 1985*, states:

> The distinction between the aims of art courses on the one hand and design courses on the other has tended to become more pronounced . . . it is now very much a case of art *or* design rather than art *and* design, as was once the case. The essential distinction between the two is that students of design will generally graduate to become designers of products for batch or mass production, whereas the artist will be concerned to express a personal message through individual works of art.

The modern design student should be concerned with the surrounding environment, alive to cultural change and stylistic nuance in accepting the challenge of communicating ideas and images clearly. Where fine art students please themselves and work to their own

36

whimsical patterns, design students work to deadlines and within the constraints of a given brief and budget. This is the crucial difference between the two areas of art school experience: graphic and industrial design students, however creative and technically skilled, are expected to solve problems which are essentially external to artistic practice. Fine artists, jealous of their autonomy, confront industrial culture with their art; designers incorporate industrial culture into their work. The idea is illustrated by the Central's description of its graphic design course: 'Not only is design today a profusion of procedures and philosophies but it is constantly changing its priorities. This is frequently due to forces outside design itself.'

Contrast this with St Martin's prospectus notes for its painting course, which:

> aims to teach painting as both a practical and philosophical activity within the current social and critical context. Students are encouraged to view painting as a search for individual expression with the recognition that both practical and theoretical considerations are intermeshed at a primary level.

Design courses are structured around fairly rigid definitions of work and technique, professional skills which are explicitly identified. Fine art courses, on the other hand, become progressively less structured, less directed, culminating in a third year of individual work towards the degree show. On the painting course at Camberwell, the

> first year is to guide each student during an important and formative phase in their development as an artist, passing from reliance on group tuition, towards a more independent position. . . . During the second and third years students are expected to have become self-sufficient and, in conjunction with their tutors, organise their own programme of work.

The old art *vs* commerce arguments are now structured *within* the education system – even on fashion courses there is disagreement as to 'whether design students should be trained as creative individuals who produce art, or as craftworkers whose main relationship should be to the mass-production industry'[22] – but it is the fine art college experience which represents the definitive expression of being and working as a Romantic artist. Unlike the design disciplines, fine art recognizes no vocational ends, and the resulting differences in attitude and application are recognized and readily commented upon by students. Graphic design students have a reputation for being more solid, more phlegmatic characters than fine art students, who relish and live out the idiosyncrasies of bohemian mythology. Never so intense, rarely so frivolous, graphic design students appear by contrast paradigms of future employability, able to deal with clients, to work in offices!

In their study of art school relationships, *Art Students Observed*, Madge and Weinberger asked a sample of both foundation and diploma level students: 'Do you think one needs talent in order to be able to do art?' Seventy-three per cent of graphic design students answered yes, 57 per cent of pre-diploma students, but only 34 per cent of fine artists. The authors add: 'A rather high proportion of fine art students either answer that they "don't know", or "don't know what talent is", or find the question "nonsensical".'[23]

Graphic design students themselves summarized the differences in approach and aspiration as follows: 'Fine artists are forced to be a bit more eccentric than others.' 'Fine artists seem deep. They are more serious and worry more about life.' And perhaps most tellingly, 'No two fine artists are the same, one cannot categorize their approach. Graphic designers have to do work that communicates to others. Fine artists can do work that communicates with itself.'

The authors also asked, 'Do you think there are basic principles in art which are teachable and which it is necessary to know?' Differences were again marked, with 77 per cent yes from graphic design students, 83 per cent yes from pre-diploma, and 44 per cent yes from fine artists. The fine art students believed that art is not taught but learned through personal discovery. Their teachers, themselves artists, trained in a similar atmosphere, often agree:

> True artists are in the end self-taught, for the work has its origins in the struggle with one's own being. So an art school should provide the conditions in which the student is most likely to discover himself.[24]

This is the civilizing ideal, the quality which sets art schools apart from the rest of higher education. The problem now is that the material conditions of art education are becoming increasingly less conducive to three years of experimentation and discovery. Students and staff may reject formal criteria, may celebrate the essentially anti-academic nature of their practice, but, as restructuring and rationalization and 'relevance' bite, the free creative personality is becoming a less and less viable option.

Art and capitalism

Art schools used to be lovely, subversive, frivolous and serious places. Now they are for training the makers of plastic telephones. (George Melly)[25]

The ideology of being an artist runs counter to utilitarianism and puts its own inflection on commercialism. The problem for art school students is that their dreams of creativity confront both an unsympathetic bureaucracy and a market place in which the soul of the artist is a commodity.

These problems have been focused since 1945 by the problem of *qualification*. British post-school education has been rationalized since the war into a three-tier system – universities offering academic degrees, polytechnics offering vocational degrees, technical colleges offering diplomas in specific skills. Art education, with its complicating concern for creativity, doesn't fit easily into any of these organizations and state policy on it has gone through two distinct phases: the post-war National Diploma in Design (NDD), built round specialist courses taught in local art colleges but designed and examined by a central bureaucracy, was replaced in 1961 by the Diploma in Art and Design (Dip. AD), which had the status and flexibility of a university degree.

The NDD was instituted in 1946 to replace a system, in force since the Board of Education's revisions of 1913, in which students began by taking preparatory and filtering drawing examinations and then entered advanced courses in industrial design, illustration, painting or modelling. Now the drawing examination gave way to the intermediate examination in Arts and Crafts and, for advanced students, the four broad areas of further study became a mass of specialized subjects. [26] The NDD structure is often remembered now as the halcyon days of art school life, when Bohemia was a viable career option and the artistic style of dress and life – fishermen's and women's jerseys and berets, the mandatory Victorian attic studio – was honed to fit the tawdry 1950s confusion of austerity and affluence. It was the time when shabby college buildings catered for fun and discovery, when artists were trained to be entertainers. The attitude is captured by Robert Macdonald who in 1958, as a 23-year-old New Zealander, enrolled at the Central on the strength of a bundle of old drawings he'd done at home: 'I was quite content to be simply an artist, doing my own thing in late Fifties London.' [27] But this is to look back through the nostalgic haze of more than a quarter of a century. At the time the NDD didn't always seem a proper qualification for the true artist: 'Finals, N.D.D., what's that? Nothing! Nothing Doing Diploma which'll earn you the glorious privilege of designin' dogfood wrappers or keepin' a roomful of delinquents in order. Where's art in that? Where's life?' [28]

Scrawdyke, David Halliwell's art school hero had his real-life counterpart in students like Eric Burdon, who equally upset his college principal by 'conducting a forum on whether students should be allowed to wear blue jeans or not', and also found his diploma useless (without college support) in getting a job. Still, this was the time when art schools became a viable step into higher education for working-class youth like Burdon, when Keith Richards could claim: 'I mean, in England, if you're lucky you get into art school. It's somewhere they put you if they can't put you anywhere else.' [29] This was the time too when money was available to buy in part-time teaching from a variety of practising artists and designers, stimulating their pupils and, crucially, providing an income for the increasing numbers of art school graduates.

This 'golden age' came to an end with the implementation of the proposals of the National Advisory Council on Art Education (NACAE) under Sir William Coldstream, which heralded a rationalization of art schools' scope and purpose. The Coldstream Report, published in 1961, recommended the abolition of the NDD, and its replacement by the Dip. AD – a more broadly based qualification, equivalent in status to a university degree, with specialized areas of fine art, graphic design, textile and fashion design, and three dimensional design. With a vague proviso for those 'temperamentally allergic to conventional education', the Dip. AD demanded revised entry qualifications of five GCE ordinary passes, of which at least three should be in acceptable academic subjects, and a minimum entry age of 18 years. To reinforce the idea that the Dip. AD was the equivalent of a university first degree, prospective students, with few exceptions, were expected, first, to complete a one year pre-diploma course, usually at their own local art college. These 'foundation' courses were to be sorting offices between secondary education and vocational and degree level courses. Sometimes according to their own inclination, usually according to teachers' perceptions of their skill and motivation, foundation courses are students' first hard experience of the practical divorce between fine arts and the rest. As Madge and Weinberger argue, such courses can be aggressively competitive – at the level of both student ego and teachers' whimsical style: 'often they just told students that their work was bloody rubbish, or that they shouldn't be there.'[30]

In 1961 the National Council for Diplomas in Art and Design (NCDAD), under Sir John Summerson, was appointed to oversee the practical implementation of the Coldstream Report and to maintain and develop standards within the colleges. Together, Coldstream and Summerson established the philosophy of art education which still prevails today. The Dip. AD gave much more freedom to individual colleges in terms of curriculum but simultaneously applied much stricter academic criteria to the selection of both students and teachers, and the problem for the NCDAD, committed to ensuring that the new courses were of the breadth and standard demanded by Coldstream, was that colleges and schools of art which had apparently been successfully training students under the old system were now incapable of meeting the higher criteria of its replacement. In 1962, eighty-seven colleges applied to run the Dip. AD courses but only twenty-nine were successful – the broad reason for rejection being non-comparability with university standards.

Art education acquired a competitive edge. More qualified students chased fewer places, and art colleges, having gained course autonomy with the NDD, were placed in direct and often unequal competition with each other. As a DES review revealed: 'Consider-able competition developed for places on the approved courses but despite the number of applicants, all of whom had completed pre-diploma courses, some principals reported difficulty in selecting sufficient entrants of the right calibre.[31] The new arrangements certainly tightened up the art school system. Despite the so-called 'loophole for the loopy' – the special entrance requirements for non-academic but artistically talented students – Coldstream represented an academic takeover of an education previously based on more intangible qualities. Romantic ideology came up against a new bureaucratic barrier.

It met a further one in Coldstream's demand, again in the name of degree equivalence, that Dip.AD study should include complementary studies and the history of art. This has remained a contentious issue in art education: students prefer to paint than take notes; they often fail to see the relevance of courses in social science. The problem was summarized by Hornsey College of Art students in 1968:

> Apart from laudably providing jobs for graduates (especially art historians) this was a perfect recipe for educational suicide. It consisted in tacking on an academic sector ('Theory') to a wide assortment of traditional forms of training in art and design (the 'Practice'), and piously hoping that it would all fit together.[32]

Despite all this, though, the Dip. AD structure has, if anything, reinforced Romantic ideology within art school practice. It's in art history classes – the incoherence of tradition – that the idea of the artist as expressive hero is most clearly articulated; a history of painters (particularly a somewhat sketchy history of painters) provides ready Romantic reference points and an easily plundered resource of heroes. More importantly, the idea of the foundation course came, in part, from representation to the Coldstream Committee by artist/teachers like Richard Hamilton, Victor Pasmore, Eduardo Paolozzi, Harry Thubron, Alan Davie and Tom Hudson. Critical of the NDD's rigidity and orthodoxy, they had constructed, from bases at the ICA and the Central, a philosophy of art teaching which allowed for the idea of 'creative education', which encouraged basic analytical experiment, and which demanded a 'clearing of the slate'.

Basic Design, as the doctrine was called, was an attempt to catch up with Modernism. In Victor Pasmore's words:

> The idea of a static system which every system must copy is not compatible with the dynamic aspirations of modern art. A modern 'basic' course, therefore, should assume a relative outlook in which only the beginning is defined and not the ened.[33]

Basic Design was part of the fabric of the Coldstream reforms; it further institutionalized the idea of the inherent individuality of artistic practice.

In 1974 the system changed again (though not its underlying logic). The Dip. AD became a BA (Art and Design). Degree-giving art colleges were absorbed into polytechnics; most of the rest simply became specialist departments in technical colleges, offering short courses in printing, photography, etc. (for clearly non-academic students like Sid Vicious).

These post-war shifts partly mark the process in which the anomalous art schools (with their idiosyncratic students) were finally placed in the higher education system. But they reflect too the difficulty of deciding what an art qualification is *for*, and, more particularly, the DES's increasing determination to have some control over the answer. Hence the general suspicion that the Coldstream proposals were pedagogically arbitrary (their educational philosophy a post-hoc rationalization), applied really for administrative convenience, in an attempt to keep some central control of art school heterogeneity.

Similar fears surround more recent reforms such as the closure of courses outside the national system of validation and the merger of inner London's senior art schools and specialized trade colleges. This attempt to create a 'powerhouse' of art and design education, is, in the words of John Barnicoat, Principal of the threatened Chelsea College, 'something dreamed up by planners – not by artists, designers or even teachers.'[34]

A darker suspicion is that the merger signals an attempt to reduce the 'overprovision' of fine art courses in London in favour of vocational ones, to switch resources from fine art freedom to new, expensive, industry-serving design technologies. Consider events at the Royal College of Art. The RCA, the original School of Design, has long been a thriving commercial enterprise, welcoming industrial commissions as well as turning out a succession of critically acclaimed fine artists – under the direction of Janey Ironside, for example, the RCA produced key fashion designers of the 1960s, like Ossie Clark and Sally Tuffin. But in 1985 the RCA provoked a particular resentment from other colleges with its advertising campaign 'recruiting' celebrities of the calibre of Richard Rogers, Sir Terence Conran, and Zandra Rhodes to senior teaching posts. 'Are we asking too much?' was the plaintive question from an institution – the country's oldest and most prestigious centre of postgraduate art and design – as it claimed to be 'entering a radical and exciting new era.' Under Jocelyn Stevens, ex-editor of *Queen* magazine, the Royal College intended, at last, to close the gap between design education and industrial application which provoked its inception in 1837. 'This must be a centre of excellence,' Stevens argued. 'We must be grappling with new techniques, new technologies, new challenges.'[35]

What were these new challenges? The Royal College was shaped as a business enterprise during the 1950s, under Robin Darwin, attracting direct commercial contracts and gaining a large percentage of its income from industrial 'programmes of research'. Darwin himself said of the shift towards sponsored design and its implications for the college as a whole:

> Of the academic changes, much the most important was my decision to pursue a policy of rigid specialisation in all fields of design, to discard responsibility towards the teaching profession and to provide courses of a thoroughly professional nature in all primary industrial design fields.[36]

Jocelyn Stevens, appointed Rector in 1984, was faced with the more immediate problem of ensuring the college's survival. The RCA had lost almost a third of its grants and was facing a severe budgetary pruning. He largely reversed this position, attracting money for capital investment, refurbishing the college's premises in Kensington Gore and warding off direct threats from the DES about the college's future. But he achieved this by cutting the faculties from five to three (leaving fine art, design and communication), by reducing the length of courses, and by centralizing shared teaching

interests where, previously, courses had enjoyed autonomy. The rationalization provoking the most concern was the closure of the environmental media course – 'the only MA opportunity', according to Malcolm Le Grice, Dean of Faculty of Art and Photography at Harrow College of Higher Education, 'for some of the most challenging of fine art graduates whose work does not fit into traditional categories'. Students within the college saw Stevens' actions as more than simple cost cutting, as an attempt to shift, radically, irreversibly, the college's curriculum and structure towards a purely commercial interest. However construed, Stevens' plans involved a dramatic shift from fine art to industrial design. As one student put it: 'the requirements of our technological society are being allowed to erode academic differences and creative diversity.'[37]

Both the London colleges merger and the recent history of the RCA illustrate the current problem for Romantic ideologists. Carried mainly through the biographical identity of the individual painter or sculptor – the paradigms of the expressive self – the creative image is under material attack as administrators and politicians attempt, once again, to redefine art school practice as 'useful' (and, these days, 'technological') design. Such attempts have shaped the whole history of art education. Can Romantic ideology survive once more to dominate art school life?

This may well depend on how effectively students can solve their own central career problem: how to organize 'autonomous' creative practice, beyond the three (or, at best, six) years of art school. Their immediate problem is access to facilities. Although fine artists generally don't need the sophisticated, expensive technical support necessary for modern design practice, canvas is not cheap, and renting studio space in the city – the natural home of the modern artist – is rarely a welcome addition to a housing benefit claim.

Art students do find work because, as a former painting student put it, they are prepared to do anything. But holding down a non-art job means becoming an evening and weekend artist, and while being a part-time sociologist or philosopher just involves boring people in pubs, being a part-time painter is hard work. And, anyway, the breadth and freedom of art education, the practices which set it and its students apart from others, have rarely endeared art graduates to employers. The independent working habits, which separate fine artists from graphic and industrial designers, do not fit easily into management structures. Industry, reversing the usual criticism, is rarely appreciative of creativity, perceiving it as a veiled threat. As one student explained, confirming industry's judgement: 'The word "Diploma" in gold letters on a scroll is not much use to you at the moment when you go for a job. It's absolutely no guarantee that you are going to be any good as a designer in some crappy industry.'[38]

The material problem for art school students is, then, the limited market for their skills – outside of artistic practice itself, beyond the confines of art school and art world, there is a limited range of applications of their talents. In Britain, teaching has been the traditional way of working in art – an acceptable compromise between independence and responsibility, a passable solution to the problem of earning 'free' time. In recent years, though, there has been a decline in art school teaching vacancies as in teaching vacancies elsewhere. Public expenditure cuts, introduced under the name of reorganization, have, in particular, reduced part-time art teaching opportunities; new graduates face increasing competition for such posts from more established, but equally hard-up artists.

The ideal remains, of course, to pursue the one vocational end of fine art training: to work as a professional painter or sculptor, to work, that is, according to the dictates of Romanticism, and as John Berger wrote about art students in the 1950s: 'Their position is logically untenable because they are being trained – nominally at least – to be painters and sculptors for whose work there doesn't begin to be any demand.'[39]

The cruel fact of the art world is that very few of the legions of yearly art school graduates will ever make more than token earnings from selling their work. For most, a mural in a provincial bank's foyer, two or three paintings hung in the local pizza house, is the only feasible goal. Check out the Census and Survey Department's figures for the occupational destinations of art school graduates: around 3 per cent are employed as 'painter, sculptor, other fine art activity'. *Working in Fine Arts*, a 1983 MSC careers information sheet, states. 'it is thought that less than 50 fine artists in Britain today actually earn a living simply through selling their work; many try but few succeed.' The problem is indicated by the fact that artists cannot get exhibitions unless they're known, locally, at least, but they can't get known unless they've exhibited. [40]

The worldly fate of the modern fine artist has always been insecure. In market terms, the shock of the new requires that the initiators of movements do indeed exhibit the art school dream of 'working for one's living by living in one's work', but there are few market prizes for coming second. Carl André's Tate Gallery bricks can only be built once – the second time around the shock effect diminishes and the investment value evaporates. In aesthetic terms, 'followers' always seem to be weaker and less 'authentic' than 'innovators', to run counter to the prime art school slogan of 'being true to oneself'. From the artist's viewpoint, art's market relations have bred both a contempt for public philistinism when their pictures don't sell and a fear of it when they do. As Garth Evans, a former Camberwell and St Martin's teacher, now living and working in New York, argues:

> In America the larger society is inclined to consider that an artist whose practice is not self-supporting is a failure. In Britain an artist is not expected to support himself by his practice. The absence of a significant market for contemporary work is the cause of much debate, frustration and regret in the British art world. Nevertheless, the art world in Britain has consistently and strenuously sought to dissociate itself from commercial activity – from the world of trade. In Britain an artist's perceived integrity may easily be compromised by commercial success. [41]

The British art school (unlike the American art school) can't be separated from the surrounding art world; art practice/art teaching/ art learning form what Evans calls 'a single continuous entity'. This partly reflects a particular attitude to commercial design – teaching is a way of preserving autonomy – but (in comparison to the USA) it also reflects a different attitude to fine art stardom. In both class and cultural terms British fine artists have always been marginal and their marginality has determined their arguments about art's function and meaning. Art schools are the natural setting for ideas of counter-culture.

Natural setting for a counter-culture

> No revolution not done for its own sake, for the joy of discovery and creation, can be worth doing, or can succeed. (Students and staff, Hornsey College of Art, 1968)

> What art and design students want is a decent education. And a job afterwards. What a large number get is anxiety and bitterness as they navigate a rigidly exclusive hierarchy of courses, colleges and exams. What the 16-year-old gets is a myth: the RCA or Slade MA who has graduated via O and A levels, foundation, and BA, subsequently becoming a practising designer, fine artist, craft businessperson (with perhaps a little part-time consultancy teaching) is statistically rare. However it is a myth which still fuels a huge and misdirected industry and provides the role model for a majority of students. [42] (Student, 1983)

The idea that artists are natural rebels gained wide cultural exposure during the student occupation of Hornsey College of Art in 1968. [43] Ostensibly caused by the proposed integration of the college into Middlesex Polytechnic, the occupation became the setting for a deeper questioning of the philosophies and purposes of education. Hornsey students had already been prominent in discussions of art training. They had initiated a meeting at the ICA in 1967 to discuss the general idea of the incorporation of art colleges into polytechnics (the feeling was that the result would be a loss of the status the Coldstream reforms had temporarily granted) and they had called a conference at the Roundhouse in July 1968 (under the name MORADE – Movement for Rethinking Art and Design Education) which, with the experience of a summer of protest, widened the debate to the nature and limits of classroom practice. The aim of the art school experience was defined as: ' . . . the creation of awareness, to allow potentially creative people to develop their attitudes, to encourage questioning, to promote discovery, to develop creative behaviour.' [44]

The critique of existing social relations of art was, in short, being posed on numerous fronts. Hornsey, opened in 1882 as a family enterprise, had received NCDAD approval for the Dip. AD in Fine Art 1 (painting with drawing), Fine Art 2 (sculpture with drawing), and Graphic Design, in the first round of post-Coldstream course reviews, and the Council later approved Hornsey's Three Dimen-

'. . . to promote discovery'

50

sional Design and Fashion/Textiles courses. But despite this relatively trouble-free weathering of the Coldstream storm, many students and some staff found the reforms distasteful. Despite the degree-equivalence status of the Dip.AD, the students lamented their lack of facilities and resented the 'luxury treatment' afforded the new 1960s universities. They disliked too the alien influence of the academic course components demanded by their 'degree', and suspected the motives of the reformers. As the Hornsey general studies lecturer Tom Nairn wrote in his opening to the staff and student account of the occupation:

> We bourgeois had been elevated as a result of the Dip.AD reforms. The improved training which was to be worthy of the new, more serious degree had to incorporate some old-style 'education' in it: book-reading, lectures, seminars, and so on. How typical of the old system to grope for progress in this.

The students saw Coldstream, overall, as an attempt to impose curricular rigidity on art colleges; the reforms were an orthodoxy in an educational sphere proud of its unorthodoxy. But the Hornsey revolt also questioned the institutional conditions of art in wider terms. What was the location of art within capitalism? Was fine art practice really marginal? How were art and design now feeding into consumer culture? This last question was particularly pertinent. In the students' own words:

> In western countries over the last few years, there has been a changing climate of sensibility, a large-scale cultural change of which we were the inheritors and would eventually be the producers.[45]

This was how Hornsey students understood their educational position, and how they perceived their wider cultural role. They'd suffered less the 'castration' of their sensibilities than other students; their senses, they argued, were more intact: 'we had not learned to live the present through books.' They had learned, rather, to live the present 'spontaneously', with an attitude to work which seemed anachronistic but which, in fact, confirmed the art school experience as vital and distinct. It was this experience, with its stress on creative autonomy, which heightened art students' perception of the 'crude materialism' of their role as potential producers of commercial culture. The danger they faced in feeding the design studios of sixties consumer society was that precious creativity would be rendered profane, autonomy squandered by affluence. In the period leading up to the occupation, staff and students had 'slid into identification with the pink plastic garden seats in the *Observer* supplement'. Both fine art and design students now wanted to create culture, not be, as they thought they had become, a 'consequence of its demands'. Through the influence of Richard Hamilton et al. the Pop art celebration of commercial practice had been fed into art education – this was via Coldstream the latest solution to the contradiction of art and capitalism. The Hornsey students, though, applied the test of Romantic ideology: the solution was the problem.[46]

The Hornsey revolt represented a moment of bohemian refusal, a style of cultural questioning which grew from the ideologies of art, work and leisure built into British art education, and it thus reflected specific institutional contradictions, but it fed into a much wider counter-culture. Hornsey students were, without bathos, able to regard themselves as a revolutionary 'vanguard'. By 1968, that is, the loose 'hippie' movement had created its own version of aesthetic revolt, working bohemian style into a general reappraisal of media form and image: 'All over Europe, America, then, artists, creative people, stepped aside into a deliberate sell-it-yourself amateurism.'[47]

Like its American counterpart, which was an ideological extension of Californian Beat culture, the British hippie scene developed around an attempt to live an aesthetic lifestyle. What distinguished sixties bohemians from previous 'angry' young men and women was their collusion with (and direct intervention in) mass media. This is best illustrated by the prodigious output of underground newspapers. Richard Neville, in *Playpower*: 'Usually, they are begun for fun, attracting a pool of underemployed creators bent on inventing a new language to communicate new ideas in a new style.'[48]

OZ and *IT*, the most significant journals – with print runs in 1968 of around 20,000 and 50,000 respectively – developed a new style of popular dissent. Looking back, what is striking is their construction as works of art: as well as being news and information sheets, they promoted a visual language. They offered themselves as imagery, drawing on the pictorial sources of symbolism and art nouveau, shaping the swirling fantasies of psychedelia. Decipher the colour overlays, deconstruct the montages, and find the tension between art and politics, 'form' and 'content'. Like 1980s-style magazines, *The Face* and *Blitz*, *OZ* and *IT* sold an idea of what life can be like – Now! – for the initiated, and lifestyle then as now was packaged as a look.

IT 38 (August/September 1968) reprinted a manifesto from the French *Le Comité d'Action*, which captured the demand always running through the underground's media trips:

> Before we can bring into being a collective and permanent creative process – not one reserved for an elite – we must put an end to the divorce between 'art' and 'life', to the distinction between artistic activities and everyday political and social ones. Must not the creative act be freed from censorship that invalidates it, and the Unconscious mind from the police state that negates it?

Part of the Romantic dilemma is whether the creative act, the ability to see in alternative and questioning ways, is a universal quality or the reserved right of the gifted, those consciously and confidently apart. The politics of the underground exploited the gaps and fusions between art and life, between cultural change and artistic innovation, but in so doing the 'counter-culture' never overcame the tension between 'distancing' and popularity, between selfish individualism and collective strategy.

Counter-cultural manifestos were most at home, most convincing, when organizing their demands around individualism, as in the following prescription from the Association of Members of Hornsey College of Art, printed in *IT* in 1968:

> The revolution remains one where imagination takes over. Conventional left-wing responses to our desperate pragmatism are useless, or worse: in an unpolitical culture like ours, it is counterproductive to repeat abstract slogans ('Get the workers out!!', 'Remember the Third World!') because the time isn't ripe for them.

Significantly, as Neville notes in *Playpower*, the underground 'while generally ambivalent to student disruptions, warmed to Hornsey

'Deconstruct the montage'

. . . somehow sensing an affinity of purpose.' The affinity was partly organized around the joint rejection of the chic bourgeois form of contemporary art – a positive tie-in between the 'academic protest' of the art schools and the wider street-based aesthetic critique of the underground. But for a crucial historical moment hippies and art students also shared other assumptions. The wonderful, inimitable quality of the alternative press was that its readers knew that a good percentage of its output was pretentious rubbish, that purchase meant 'wasting 2/6 on the biggest load of boring old scrofulous crap to come my way in many a long day', as one letter stated in OZ. But this complaint missed the point, which was the constant emphasis on confusion and change, on innovation as an end, on the pressing need to stay one cultural jump ahead, on nonsense as a valid stance. OZ and IT were, whatever else, fun. Reading them required the skills of distraction. As Neville said:

> There is one quality which enlivens both the political and cultural denominations of youth protest; which provides its most impor-tant innovation; which has the greatest relevance for the future; which is the funniest, freakiest and the most effective. This is the element of play . . . [49]

For the hippies, play had to be Now, realizable through the whole of their cultural life. This is why the late sixties bohemian counter-culture put the full weight of its creative energies into the institu-tional reorganization of the media, why the aesthetic strategies of cultural change involved posters, printing, publishing, bookshops, music, film and video. In these areas work could be transformed into 'substitute play', activities where 'every Monday morning is a Saturday night'. Media practice was, as Neville realized, modernized art practice, dissolving the work/leisure distinction: there were no Positions Vacant columns in the underground press. And the area in which this creative stance was worked through most thoroughly, which transmitted Romantic ideology most effectively into popular culture, was music.

On May Day 1983, Pop artist Peter Blake appeared on Radio 1's My Top Twelve. Blake's choice of music for his imaginary LP was conventional but had unusual personal angles: alongside Chuck Berry, Jerry Lee Lewis and Gladys Knight, was the title track from

Sgt Pepper (Blake designed the cover), the Who's *Who Are You* (in honour of longtime friendship with Pete Townshend and Blake's influence on the Who's original costume design), and a song from Ian Dury called 'Peter the Painter' (Blake taught Dury in the early sixties). In between tracks, Blake casually linked the worlds of pop and art. In the late sixties, he recalled, major pop and rock stars thronged London galleries, discussing ideas with the artists; Sam the Sham and the Sir Douglas Quintet were essential art school listening then (as jazz and blues had been a decade earlier). Kinks songs, Blake said, mirrored his own art concerns – he liked the Kinks because he shared Ray Davies's obsession with an imagery taken from everyday elements of British culture – London sunsets, the village green, the taxman, the commuter, the followers of fashion. The biographical references of his chosen tracks were not past emotional states (pop records' usual historical referents) but highpoints of cultural innovation, a sense of things being significant to their time.

Why should 'significance' enter pop rhetoric – once concerned solely with sentimentality, the language of love, dancing and having a good time? We discuss this in proper detail in chapter 3, but some summary points should be made here. The crucial shift was that, by 1967, pop's established sense of escapism seemed inadequate to the dominant cultural mood of optimism. Music still confirmed the desires of youth, but those desires were changing: music was needed, now, to symbolize and express the feeling of a new generation that it could embody real cultural and political change. Pop became rock and musicians redefined their practice. 'Art' rock – the musical background to the counter-culture – was not concerned to 'reflect' the ideas of a wider community, it was a source of missionary zeal about consumption, leisure and style.

British hippie musicians – from 'psychedelics' like Hendrix and Cream to 'progressives' like Soft Machine and Pink Floyd – laid claim to a special knowledge and the models for their claims – pop stars as seers – were found in poetry and painting. Just as the counter-cultural media generally constructed their interventions around a modernized image of artistic practice, so the new rock form defined itself against pop commercialism by reference to Romantic ideology. Musicians delved into the store rooms of art history and plundered its stars. They began to identify themselves with art

'Pop and rock stars thronged the London galleries'

heroes like Van Gogh, art movements like Dada and Surrealism. Art
had always claimed the right to shape culture, rock stars now in-
sisted too on the right, as Ruskin said dismissively of Whistler, 'to
fling a pot of paint in the public's face'. Musicians affected a self-
conscious bohemian style, bohemians saw rock as a noisy new
means of self-expression, and the rock audience required new skill to
understand the symbolism, the nuances of Romantic style. Reading
Blake's *Sgt Pepper* sleeve – name the faces, spot the cannabis, decode
the lyrics – was like reading the underground press. This was a skill
which could easily be acquired – from friends, from the neighbourhood dealer, even across the counter – but it was always constructed

around a sense of difference from the 'mass' pop audience. Art rock was 'superior' at all levels, and fans took seriously the prime Romantic axiom: the philistines had to be kept out, left at the doors of Middle Earth and UFO.

To an extent, of course, the counter-cultural milieu simply provided a research department for record companies and delivered them an audience ideologically committed to 'the new'. As Miles noted in *IT* 38: 'The problem of people "selling out" will possibly never be solved at this stage. . . . It is regrettable that the U/G is thus a "test-bed" for new sounds and talent and receives none of the rewards.' The resulting questions – What was musicians' attitude to their public? How should they treat success? – had been art school issues for years. At one level the art/audience relationship was solved in the name of 'community'. Piblokto's 1970 LP, *The Art School Dance Goes on Forever*, got the point. This was jokey, exclusive rock (Piblokto's leader, Pete Brown, wrote the obscure lyrics for Cream) which celebrated a specific collective attitude: the art school combination of ironic hedonism and a commitment to the weird. Pink Floyd, similarly, may have found fame playing hippie venues like Middle Earth, UFO and the Marquee, but they'd already served their apprenticeship on the London art college circuit. Where else could they go? For thirty years now the local art school dance has been the social centre of drugs and in-sounds and hip style, the setting for art school students to experience their own exclusivity and for 'the kids', the local would-be faces, to be initiated into Bohemia. A rock generation after Pink Floyd, the Sex Pistols' first gig was an art school dance too; here was the only audience that would appreciate the aesthetics of incompetence, would dance or jeer with glee at the inversion of style.

The first sociological analysts of punk made sense of it in subcultural terms, as the semantics of street youth. Punk was the rattling sound of 'the empty life of the jobless teenager':

> It is about people having access to their own music because the music is within the reach of their own competence. As soon as a punk rock group starts to succeed, it will be dead; it will have moved outside of the milieu which gives reason to its very existence. You can't play dole-queue rock and eat well at the same time. [50]

ABOUT COLLAGE: TOURIST ATTRACTION

'The nuances of Romantic style'

Now we've all seen *The Great Rock 'n' Roll Swindle* and such comments seem touchingly naive – academics fell for Malcolm McLaren's schemes as surely as the media moralists. The subcultural analysis was irresistible – punk fitted the bill of authentic working-class angst, a welcome return to rock 'n' roll's roots after the confusing interlude of art rock and counter-culture, an obvious 'solution' to unemployment, the death of the teenager and the loss of youth's consuming power. Dick Hebdige was one of the few commentators to grasp the point of punk more clearly, to go beneath the symbolism of 'the pogo as the high-rise leap':

59

Such readings are both too literal and too conjectural. They are extrapolations from the sub-culture's own prodigious rhetoric, and rhetoric is not self-explanatory: it may say what it means but it does not necessarily 'mean' what it 'says'. In other words, it is opaque: its categories are part of its publicity.[51]

And punk's original rhetoricians came from the art room not the streets. It was at art college in the late 1960s, for example, that Malcolm McLaren first realized the significance of fashion and style as a blank cultural canvas on which political ideas could be stencilled:

It's very important because I work with human beings. That's the only difference. Instead of using the canvas, I have to use human beings. It's just the work I've chosen to do – not through any personal choice originally, but what I decided was my best path to follow when I left art school. What I could automatically get a response from quickly seemed to be fashion because of my knowledge and background. It was a subject I harnessed myself to and used.[52]

The Sex Pistols had nothing to 'say' to Bob Harris or his *Whistle Test* viewers; but, equally, they had no desire to *please*. If the pop industry sold prepackaged excitement, punk sold the aesthetics of boredom and the politics of street incredibility. Punk's artist-designers took conceptual art into lifestyle and offered not a solution to non-work but a solution to leisure: play on the dole. Punk modernized the rhetoric, but the message suggested sixties bohemia. Jamie Reid's slogan might have been 'Never trust a hippie' but he and McLaren were the hippies not to be trusted, and McLaren, at least, laughed all the way in and out of the bank. The pose was radical chic aesthetics, the politics of creative subversion. Authenticity was a matter of strategy. We will discuss the details of this in chapter 4. The point to stress here is that punk's most profound message was about do-it-yourself creativity – this ideal remained as punk itself became another capitalist spectacle.

What both hippie counter-culture and punk Bohemia did, then, was direct the ideological concerns of artistic practice into rock and pop. Art school Romanticism was translated into the terms of popular culture: bohemian solutions seemed relevant, briefly, to the ways 'the kids' made sense of their everyday lives. The sociological assumption was (and is) that hippie youth culture was a middle-class response to affluence, punk a working class response to decay, but both responses were mediated by art students and articulated ideas of labour and leisure which reflected art students' own class confusion. The nervous tension of both hippie and punk Bohemians arose not directly from their untenable positions but from the usual contradictions of avant-garde art: how to balance public success against private 'truth', how to communicate the aesthetic of refusal. As Peter Fuller has suggested: 'It is only a mild exaggeration to say that now no one wants fine artists, except fine artists, and that neither they nor anyone else have the slightest idea what they should be doing, or for whom they should be doing it.' [53]

This problem has haunted modern fine art practice: the problem of a 'freedom' lacking tangible material, social hooks. Artists and art students are marginal in a class sense, but they're also marginal culturally, as fine art has been trivialized as a cultural practice. Art is no longer central to the way most people make sense of the world. Even in the simple production of essential visual images modern art has been replaced by technology. Their irrelevance has granted artists a greater practical autonomy – the power to define the nature of human perception exemplified by the drift into abstract expressionism and conceptual introversion – but it has also loosened their cultural roots. Fine artists' individual claims to 'vision' have become weaker as fine art's pure investment value has soared. It was this sense of cultural marginality that underlay nineteenth-century aestheticism, 'art for art's sake', and determined the emergence of the modernist style. As society needed art less, artists began to examine their own practice, the means of representation itself. The resulting struggle with marginality is most vividly illustrated by avant-garde stances in the first decades of the twentieth century, which took Romantic ideas of the artist as visionary to the extreme: change artistic practice an social conditions will follow suit! In Robert Hughes's words:

> The essence of the avant-garde myth is that the artist is a precursor; the truly significant work of art is one that prepares the future. The focus of culture, on the other hand, tends to treat the present (the living artist) as the culmination of the past. [54]

Avant-garde art revolved around ideas of personality and cult, played on a sense of difference. The most notorious groups, Dada and the Surrealists, shifted the focus of art away from what is produced to the reaction to it. Attempting to destroy the bourgeois idea of cultural autonomy, the aura of art, they created a new aesthetic quality which Walter Benjamin called art's 'uselessness for contemplative immersion'.

Sixties counter-culture used this model very deliberately. The best underground events (the festival, the happening ...) were spontaneous, impermanent, beyond preservation (until *Woodstock – The Movie* destroyed Woodstock the Festival in an endless replay). Initiated originally by artists like Oldenberg, Jim Dine and Yoko Ono, 'happenings' drew on Dada and Surrealist ideas of the liberating public effects of the free-play of the unconscious. Attempts to negate and distort the formal limitations of artistic practice, happenings made art an 'event' in which artistic action and audience reaction were part of the design. As Jeff Nuttall says, these artistic intentions became part of the sixties pop style:

> Clearly when the Who, a particularly violent pop group, went berserk and smashed up their amplifying equipment, and that was subsequently kept in as part of the show, when the Move obliterated effigies of politicians as they played, there was a close connection between the popular music world and the previously separate world of art. [55]

Pete Townshend's guitar smashing was, indeed 'inspired' by the auto-destructive artist Gustav Metzger (see chapter 3), but the crucial point was that the audience, in both the formal art happening and the happening-influenced pop event, became props or accessories to the artist/musicians' intentions. This was even more obvious in early punk concerts in which the 'shock effect' often meant violence, a perpetual spitting and snarling between players and listeners. Punk fanzines, Dadaesque manifestos in comparison to the underground's Symbolist and Surrealist jokes, drifted in and out of magazine racks, dripped slogans down the walls, sensible to the initiated, disgusting to everyone else. The tactic was to court disdain – as Dada participant Hans Richter remembered: 'Our feeling of freedom from rules, precepts, money and critical praise, a freedom for which we paid the price of an excessive distaste and contempt for the public, was a major stimulus.'[56]

Dada's legacy was its celebration of spontaneity – it introduced irony and fun into the attack on the bourgeois idea of art – but avant-garde artists also take themselves seriously. Dada and Surrealist artists were, in part, skilled technicians who created and performed for a knowing audience, a community of the converted, but in attacking the institutions of art, the spurious notion of 'autonomy', 'their effort was not to isolate themselves, but to reintegrate themselves and their art into life. It is no accident that the active, even aggressive artistic manifesto – an address to fellow artists and society – became the preferred medium of expression for the avant-garde artist of the twentieth century.' In Bürger's words:

> Aestheticism had made the distance from the praxis of life the content of works. The praxis of life to which Aestheticism refers and which it negates is the means–end rationality of the bourgeois everyday. Now it is not the aim of the avant-gardists to integrate art into *this* praxis. On the contrary, they assent to the aestheticians' rejection of the world and its means–ends rationality. What distinguishes them from the latter is the attempt to organise a new life praxis from a basis in art. In this respect also, Aestheticism turns out to have been the necessary precondition of the avant-gardiste intent. Only an art the contents of whose individual works is wholly distinct from the (bad) praxis of the existing society can be the centre that can be the starting point for the organisation of a new life praxis.[57]

The problem, as Bürger goes on to suggest, is that the development of the culture industry since Dada has brought about a 'false elimination between art and life'. What progressive rock and punk musicians couldn't avoid, forty years later, was to become 'popular', to be placed, that is, in an established 'entertaining' role. The potential audience was too large, the means of transmission and consumption too sophisticated and public to permit coded subversion. By the mid-1960s, cults couldn't avoid becoming a 'mass'. The avant-garde challenge was to keep art beyond the reach of the philistine, the 'collector', but now the significant consuming group was more youthful, more willing to accept shock as pleasure, provocation as leisure.

Avant-garde ideology seemed to become obsolete with affluence, a shift described by American critic Harold Rosenberg: 'There are no objective issues in contemporary culture, and there is no need to take a position. To champion new works because they are new is as orthodox as to attack them for the same reason.'[58]

Despite continuing bourgeois suspicion of artistic intentions, the newness, the modernity of a work of art was by the end of the 1950s its major selling point – the hook the buying public could most easily grasp. Modernism had become the natural way of seeing, capitalism's official culture, and by the 1960s even avant-garde art (apparently, following Duchamp, unconsumable) had become a commodity – as a label, a record, an idea.

If 1960s affluence had any reality beneath the political myths, it involved a public celebration of consumer culture. And now art imitated life: Pop art stars like Andy Warhol honoured consumer culture too. For Warhol, Culture is Advertising, Advertising creates Fashion, and now Fashion was Art – his aim was to complete the circle that made the innovatory imagery of the twentieth century avant-garde a part of the High Fashion discourse. Warhol, suggested American critic Gregory Battcock, 'correctly foresaw the end of painting and became its executioner'.[59]

But Pop art didn't so much kill painting as invalidate the avant-garde pose. This was a paradoxical outcome (and a sign of the times) because the first generation of American Pop artists had used mass media imagery in their (high) art work precisely to challenge conventional visual tastes and perception. And their initial effect was both shocking ('What's an image like *this* doing in a gallery?') and elitist (only the properly schooled spectator and critic could 'see through' the image to the arguments about art value). But Pop art radicalism was soon invalidated by market forces themselves – the painters involved became bestsellers – and incorporated instead in the British approach to Pop. Here artists' 'superior' vision informed a kind of anthropology: all of society's practices, all visual culture was now valid as 'art'. In Lawrence Alloway's words: 'the mass media were entering the work of art and the whole environment was being regarded, reciprocally, by the artists as art, too.' The critical distance of the marginal artist had gone. Pop culture was Pop art, Pop art was pop culture (for further discussion of this see chapter 3).[60]

64

Avant-garde artists had long sought liberation through art; now the slogan was packaged in the name of lifestyle. Revolution through art fitted the logic of affluent consumerism well. The cult became the customer and the artist became the star. Being a star means playing on a sense of difference, becoming a pop and rock star involves selling the difference to the masses: superior vision and technique in the late sixties, the aesthetics of the taunting obscenity in the mid-seventies. Art school-trained musicians took ingredients from the avant-garde but changed the recipe, stirred in Pop art ideas too – what we got was not art *vs* commerce, but commerce as art, as the canvas for the musician's creativity, individuality, style.

But to understand this fully we need to look at one more factor in the art school context, the rejigging of the ideological distinction (still clear in the 1960s, as we've seen) between 'free' fine artists and 'hack' designers. The uneasy art school coexistence of such distinct slants on cultural production has always been experienced by students themselves in terms of identity. Where fine artists could define their 'marginality' in traditional Romantic language, design students had no clear models of their creative value. Their training stressed *usefulness*: 'Well, lad,' Eric Burdon was greeted by his principal after he'd completed his course, 'I suppose you'll be off to London to see if you can find a place in a commercial house.' And, at least since the Bauhaus, even the most avant-garde design ideas have been interpreted as functional. The stress on the new translates readily into the capitalist idea of competitive modernism and consumer fad. Both in classroom and career, then, the difference between art and design is experienced as a difference in working practice – artists struggling alone with their materials, designers serving a production team. As a 1983 careers guide from the Manpower Services Commission put it:

> Art and design are closely linked and both call for a combination of creativity with practical skills. However, in career terms the prospects for, and routes pursued by, designers tend to be very different. Designers, typically, work to a brief provided by other people where the finished product will come off a 'production line' or a printing press. Artists and craftsmen by contrast work on their own and for themselves both designing and making the finished product. [61]

As we have already seen, though, the problem for both govern-ment and educators is that designers' collaborative practice is rarely given much art school prestige. Designers *are* artists and the fine art aesthetic has in the past been too strong for there to be a convincing alternative, design-based ideal – the 1982 report, *The Arts and Higher Education*, funded by Leverhulme and the Gulbenkian Foundation, concluded that this was because fine art was too influential in the fill-ing of teaching posts, and too alluring in its vision of what it meant to be 'a professional artist'. The problem had been analysed in the same way in the 1970 report of the NACAE, which informed the then Education Secretary, Margaret Thatcher, that foundation courses in art schools 'over-emphasized' fine art skills and practice, limiting the courses' claimed diagnostic function in other areas.

This is to recast the story we've already told – no longer fine art-ists defending their position against the demands of industry, but designers succumbing to the blandishments of fine art. Misha Black suggests that even in Victorian art schools:

> The fine artists were the aristocrats and those who once unques-tioningly accepted their less exalted occupation as industrial art-isans in the useful arts began to escape from their supposed ser-vitude by moving from industry-based design to the hand crafts of ceramics, silversmithing, weaving, stained glass, furniture-making, book-binding and those other crafts which share a historical relationship with the fine arts. By the mid-1930s the process had been completed. A few schools of art and crafts paid lip service to the needs of industry and of 'commercial art'; none in Britain provided an effective education in design. [62]

The recurring criticism of art education has, therefore, been that it takes fine art practice to be the summit of achievement and design to be a career for 'failures'. And if British industry suffers from this situation so do designers, because their problem can be phrased in reverse terms: British industry (despite the best efforts of the Design Council) does not understand design practice; designers are peri-pheral to the manufacturing process and have low status in industry too – they're compelled to work within established paradigms rather than enabled to create new ones. Their lack of prestige in the art world becomes a lack of authority in the work place. As one

British designer, now working in Europe puts it: 'In Britain, managers take a moralistic attitude towards design: it is something to be added if there is time and money because you ought to. In Europe, businessmen use design to make money.'[63] David Maroni, Director of External Relations for British Olivetti, argues that the difference in commercial attitudes towards design reflects employers' differing willingness to take risks. Asked whether graduates' work is used more effectively abroad, he replied: 'They are given far more chance to express themselves with no holds barred abroad. A designer needs freedom to express himself, to try out various things, otherwise he's stifled.'[64] This is to counter a hundred years of argument from the Department of Education. In his time there, for example, Sir Keith Joseph was always insistent that the failure of British industry to present an exciting design image was the fault of art schools' 'expressive' prejudices.

But, by then, this complaint seemed somehow to miss the point. By the early 1970s the central role of fine art training in design education was being questioned even in art schools and in some had been all but dropped. Fine art and design had been divided administratively and indeed most college course guides insist that the split is now absolute. This is illustrated by the growing number of DATEC/BTEC courses validated since 1979 by the Design and Art Committee of the Technician Education Council. By 1983, over 200 of these courses, predominantly based in colleges of Further Education, had been approved. These offer a route (an alternative to foundation courses, although regarded with suspicion by most colleges) into traditional art education but they were primarily established as vocational courses, with curricula and exercises geared to suit the 'real world' of design and advertising. They concentrate, in particular, on contemporary production methods, on the new technologies of imagery and communication – what have gone are the old prescriptions of art and design harmony, Morris's idea of the 'organic relationship' between the designer and manufacturer, and the Bauhaus stress on the craft workshop (all of which had fed into foundation course ideology). Such courses may thus avoid the 'corrupting' influence of fine art ideas, but, as the latest attempt to *professionalize* design education, to improve designers' status, put their own sort of value on creativity. Richard Boston, with characteristic art school snootiness, describes the manoeuvre:

> In the old days commercial artists were little men with Brylcreem-
> ed hair, toothbrush moustaches and sleeve garters, and were dis-
> tinguished from commercial travellers only by their bow ties.
> What they did was something very clever. They changed their
> name. After years of being commercial artists they all woke up
> one morning and announced they were graphic designers. [65]

It is as simple as that! Redefine design to serve popular culture
rather than manufacturing industry (designers as the real Pop artists)
and commercial art becomes successful and street credible –
designers rather than artists are the cultural icons in *The Face* and
now even have their own gallery space, in the Boilerhouse. The
competitive individualism fine art and fine-art-influenced design
education cultivates may not train graduates well for traditional industrial activity (the Joseph point) but it blends perfectly with the
commercial careerism, the profit ideology of popular cultural production (as Sir Terence Conran was the first designer to realize).
Advertising, after all, where design imagery is most visible, is an
occupation in which art school graduates have always had a career.
This is the real twentieth-century profession of skilled image-
makers, the domain of commercial activity where consumer choice
is a matter of aesthetics as well as finance. Advertising uses artifice
rather than art – art techniques and references employed as a means
to a commercial end – but within the advertising studio, Romanticism rules, with personality cults and celebrity status (and large
salaries) organized around the latest creative genius. As Edward
Lucie-Smith states:

> The advertising agency is the last refuge of the creative tantrum on
> a grand scale – the kind that prima donnas used to have in the days
> of Melba and Tetrazinni. It is also, I think, the one remaining place
> where people still retain the illusion that 'high art' differs from any
> other kind. [66]

In the twenty years since Lucie-Smith's comments the only obvious
change in the advertising industry is its bigger scale, a reflection of
the increasing business dependence on skilled image-makers, profits
on style. In Deyan Sudjic's words, design has become 'anything that

makes things sell', and design ideology has therefore been integrated into the sales conventions of multinational capital. The designers' success, like the pop star's, can only be measured by the aesthetic of the market place.

> All this has had the effect of eliminating much of the character of everyday artefacts and the tradition of unconscious design, shaped by those engineers and entrepreneurs who have in the past consistently been able to turn out products, signs and buildings with an indelible personality. In their place we have what is very often a fashion-led replacement or an arch, knowing manipulation of the clichés of modern design. [67]

Warhol's parodies of advertising's commercial/art promises got the point. The best advertising sells the illusion of creative consumer choice, the individuality of both product and buyer; the most penetrating campaigns sell instant style, the promise that the buyer is unique. Everyone, for a market moment, can be an artist.

Modern advertising thus continues where Pop art left off; filling in the gaps, revising the references. Advertising and fashion, the style industries, always offered art school graduates a lucrative escape route from the artistic proletariat, but now this is a route to personal celebrity too. C. More Tone (Chris Morton), Stiff Records designer until 1982 and now freelance, remarks that 'it's no good getting frustrated with the limitations, 'cos I know I have to live with them, and I couldn't really make a living selling actual paintings – and I'd probably get bored without having deadlines to keep,' but this account of his situation is less interesting than its appearance in *Blitz*. [68] How many record buyers in the 1950s or 1960s cared who designed their packages? Recognized Andy Warhol's jazz sleeve touch?

The face, *Blitz* and *i – D*, the style council of contemporary pop culture, market art school sensibility in a way in which creativity, commentary and commerce have become indistinguishable. With their inner coherence – the same imagery runs through text and advertising and display – these magazines are the most revealing postmodern texts. Essential posing material for home stylists from Sydney to San Francisco, they have become journals of international art, chronicles of a new celebrity system. But their art school translation of avant-garde cultism into *pop* stardom is uniquely British. As Robert Elms has said, style is 'our national sport now and you have to get the complete kit'. It is 'the knowledge that stops us from being Americans'. [69]

3
THE ROCK BOHEMIANS

. . . and they've got a place for her at Edinburgh Art College, her grant is in the pipeline, and there's no stopping her. The city glitters. Duffel coats and striped college scarves, drainpipes and jazz, bell-bottoms and the Beatles: the last of the Bohemians, the first of the Rock Generation. (Alison Fell)[1]

When he was discharged from his Guards regiment at the end of the Second World War, Humphrey Lyttelton enrolled as a student at the Camberwell School of Arts and Crafts. On Monday nights he'd go to the Red Barn at Barnehurst, Kent, 'a drear, dull, thirties-built suburb', for an evening of New Orleans jazz – first a lecture and record recital, then live music from George Webb's Dixielanders. In his autobiography Lyttelton remembers how determined these 'real' jazzers were to distinguish themselves from Britain's pre-war dance band musicians. They were contemptuous of band uniforms, stage compères, novelty numbers; they cultivated a deliberate image of no image, dressing down, basking in their lack of 'professionalism'. They modelled their playing on black rather than white American performers, and their very amateurism (George Webb and several of his band members were full-time workers at the nearby Vickers-

Armstrong plant) was taken to guarantee both their resistance to commercial pressures and their proletarian sympathies – their initial central London concerts were promoted by the Young Communist League's Challenge Jazz Club. But this was a meritocratic set-up and old Etonian Lyttelton soon became a Dixielander too, before leaving, in November 1947, to form his own band (taking Wally Fawkes, ex-Sidcup Art School, with him). Jim Godbolt, the Dixielanders' then manager, comments: 'It's certain that there would have been a [trad jazz] "revival" in Britain without Webb-Lyttelton but this strange flowering of an alien culture in a drear-dull London suburb, with an upper-crust gent and a band of factory workers, spearheaded a movement that spread throughout the country with quite sensational results.'[2]

Godbolt is referring only to the 1950s jazz movement here, but this story contains many of the threads that were woven into the even more sensational 1960s rock movement – 'authenticity' measured (against commercialism) by white Britons' successful imitations of black Americans; music as a self-conscious suburban cult; musicians from different class backgrounds coming together in a white collar milieu which defined itself as proletarian. In the sixties this milieu was to be art school hang-outs as such; in the forties art school musicians like Lyttelton and Fawkes (and art school jazz fans like Peter Blake) still needed to set out in the evenings to a rhythm club. Blake, who went to the Dartford Rhythm Club while a young student at Gravesend School of Art in the late 1940s, remembers the two worlds as separate: 'What I was doing was going into art school and being an art student then going home and being a youth, going to jazz clubs.'[3] But these clubs, rooms above pubs, people's bedrooms even, where serious young men (and a few young women) gathered to play and discuss records, established musical attitudes which were essential to the art school musicians of the 1960s. Pretty Thing Dick Taylor, who reached Sidcup Art College about twenty years after Wally Fawkes,

> found that the students' common room contained an essential
> item, in constant use, and probably found in every other common
> room in [the British art school] at that time – a record player.
> Amid the inevitable trad Dixieland and modern jazz records that

were played by duffel coated enthusiasts, would also be found those of black r 'n' b artists, whose records were starting to appear in the specialist shops.[4]

The continuity between rhythm club and art school culture is suggested geographically too. The main centre of the rhythm club movement (started by *Melody Maker* in 1933) was London, which by 1935 had clubs in the following areas: Central London, North Middlesex, Croydon, Forest Gate, Ealing, East Ham, Barking, Richmond, Willesden, Sutton, Walthamstow, Greenwich, Uxbridge, Edgware, Muswell Hill, Lewisham, Edmonton, South Norwood, Carshalton, Hornsey, Wembley, Woodford Green. 'The student will observe', wrote Francis Newton in 1959, 'the absence of Rhythm Clubs in Hampstead, Kensington or Chelsea.'[5] But the student today will observe too the similarity of this list to the list of suburban art schools that fed the 1960s London r & b and rock scene: Sidcup (Phil May, Dick Taylor, Keith Richards), Ealing (Ron Wood, Pete Townshend, Thunderclap Newman, Freddy Mercury), Kingston (Eric Clapton, Keith Relf, Sandy Denny, John Renbourne, Tom McGuiness), Camberwell (Syd Barrett), Wimbledon (Jeff Beck), Hornsey (Ray Davies, Roger Glover), Croydon (Mike Vernon), Sutton (Jimmy Page), Harrow (Charlie Watts) and Hammersmith (Cat Stevens). These musicians may have started something new – British beat – but they were part of a cultural tradition.

The story we're going to tell in this chapter is straightforward: how in the 1960s art school students became rock and roll musicians and in doing so inflected pop music with bohemian dreams and Romantic fancies and laid out the ideology of 'rock' – on the one hand a new art form, on the other a new community. But what interests us in this story are the confusions that arose as musicians developed different strategies to retain their creative autonomy when they become implicated in commercial routine. One such strategy was 'progressive' rock. Groups like Pink Floyd presented themselves as performers and composers 'above' normal pop practice and, by the early 1970s, were so successful in selling high seriousness (for their fans this was the most *flattering* pop form) that any contradictions between creative and market forces seemed to be resolved. If so, this was at the expense of any notion of non-conformity – by now a Pink Floyd concert was a showbiz spectacle like any other – and so for other musicians (exemplified in the early 1970s by Roxy Music) the artistic challenge was to seize control of the commercial process itself, to subvert pop from the inside. Art-pop (inspired more or less directly by Pop art) meant not individual expression (like art-rock) but the manipulation of signs.

As even this summary suggests, one of the difficulties in getting this story straight is the imprecision of the crucial descriptive terms – 'pop' and 'rock' have long been loaded labels, made to mean different things to different people. What's at issue is the opposition authenticity/artifice; what's impossible is to make the distinction stick. 'True' expression always means faking it (Eric Clapton didn't grow up black, American or poor and Bruce Springsteen long sinced ceased to be a working man) while even the most excessive Vegas routines depend on conventions of sincerity. Authenticity and its discontents and artifice and its uneasy pleasures define capitalist culture generally (see chapter 5) but they are particular potent sources of value in British popular music, perhaps because our early experience of industry, empire and the metropolis undermined all folk music forms. In the USA roots and rural musics still have presence and a rock Romanticism has developed (the populist line from rockabilly through Credence Clearwater Revival and The Band to Springsteen) that celebrates the star as democratic representative, speaking *for* the culturally dispossessed. Romantics in Britain speak only for themselves, and seek, usually in vain, to state their differences from everyone else.

Art schools in the 1950s: the making of a Bohemia

At the start of her 1958 novel, *The Bell*, Iris Murdoch describes her heroine thus:

> Dora was still very young, though she vaguely thought of herself as past her prime. She came of a lower middle-class London family. Her father had died when she was nine years old, and her mother, with whom she had never got on very well, had married again. When Dora was eighteen she entered the Slade school of art

with a scholarship . . . The role of an art student suited Dora. It was indeed the only role she had ever been able wholeheartedly to play. She had been an ugly and wretched schoolgirl. As a student she grew plump and peach-like and had a little pocket money of her own, which she spent on big multi-coloured skirts and jazz records and sandals.

In her memoirs of art school life in the early 1950s Mary Quant describes her hero, Alexander Plunket Greene, in contrasting terms:

He lived in Chelsea; he had a house all to himself because his mother was convalescing in the country; he played jazz on the trumpet; was thought to take drugs; and boasted the wildest parties in London.[6]

These were the two sides of the 1950s art school student image – on the one hand, earnest, slightly dreary, student 'bohemians' (whom Julian MacLaren-Ross and his 1940s friends called 'Slithy Toves'); on the other hand, the Chelsea Set, idle, worldly, flamboyant.

It is unlikely that Dora and Alexander would have had much to do with each other had they been at the same college (he was actually at Goldsmiths) but they shared a taste for jazz, and a sense that the artist's life justified unconventional gestures which were, in turn, a guarantee of superior sensibility. Art school students in those days distanced themselves from both the respectability of their varied middle-class backgrounds and from the 'trivial' commercial pleasures of the masses. Jazz was art school music on both counts – as a form of emotional and physical expression subversive of polite concert hall tradition and as something more complex, truthful and interesting than the Light Programme and the High Street hit parade.

The peculiarity of jazz in Britain is that something understood as a folk form, live music for dancing and community entertainment, became a recording cult, music for collectors, for an elite of jazz students, critics, musicologists and discographers. Solemnity not excitement defined true jazz fans, who self-consciously distanced themselves from the general public and were suspicious when anyone like Louis Armstrong became popular. Humphrey Lyttelton suggests that British fans thus distorted the music's meaning but, at the time, he shared some of their basic prejudices, attributing the sales success of Bill Haley's 'Rock Around the Clock' to its plugging by the BBC, and dismissing rock 'n' roll as simply the mass produced 'trash' end of the real blues. [7]

In the 1940s and early 1950s jazz and art school worlds came together not so much because art schools produced jazz musicians (Monty Sunshine was the only notable artist-turned-performer besides Lyttelton and Fawkes) as because they provided jazz fans. Paul Oliver, writing in the 1957 *Jazz Monthly* ('the magazine of intelligent jazz appreciation') noted the particular interest of art students in jazz (and the importance of college venues like Camberwell, Goldsmiths and the RCA for London's jazz musicians) and suggested obvious reaons for it – 'the well-known attraction of the art student to the socially unconventional and unacceptable'; jazz's 'romantic appeal as the music of a minority group'. But overriding such loose emotional ties was a more explicit argument, then being developed in the ICA's controversial series of jazz lectures: jazz was the musical equivalent of modern art, a musical form, that is, which had 'broken with the orthodoxy of the past as emphatically as did the contemporaneous painting and sculpture of the first decade of the century'.

> In collective improvisation there exists a bond between musicians which demands a unity of spirit, a reciprocity of ideas which yet permits the self-expression of the individual, and in a period when artistic schools of thought are inclined to diverge more and more from the slower moving progression of public taste, such simultaneous unity and freedom is for the artist eminently desired. To the Romantic and Expressionist artist, particularly, the element of improvisation, of spontaneous creation and swift, almost intuitive interpretation of a theme which is present in jazz of all periods, seems an echo of the extempore nature of much of his own work. [8]

The point is not that 1950s art school students adapted jazz to their own ideologies of creativity, but, rather, that there already existed an interpretation of jazz (developed in the pre-war rhythm clubs) that fed into art students' post-war understanding of their cultural position and activity. Jazz mattered to the lower-middle-class pupils of suburban and provincial colleges, in particular, not for its wildness, exoticism or shock value (the supposed qualities of black music embraced by upper-class jazz lovers) but for its *seriousness*. Such seriousness was reinforced in the 1950s by the rise of modern jazz and its association with existentialism and the formal avant-garde (the be-bop musicians themselves, Jeff Nuttall once suggested, could be seen as 'cod-bohemians', parodying their scholarly fans in sombre dress, horn-rim spectacles and goatee beards, perfecting a 'cool', unexpressive stage demeanour).[9]

The 1950s trad *vs* mod debate cut across jazz fans everywhere but it had paradoxical effects in the art schools. The unexpected trad 'boom' at the end of the decade meant new sorts of sales package for previously purist performers and to the general public it seemed obvious that these new bands in their self-mocking suits (Acker Bilk et al.) had emerged from the Arts Ball, the world of explicitly surrealist and comic art college entertainers like the Alberts and Temperance Seven and, later, the RCA-based Bonzo Dog Band (one of the Beatles' earliest performances, in 1959, was on a dressed-up float at the Liverpool Arts Ball). But despite such public jokiness, the typical art school jazz fan remained deadly serious. The jazz attitude fostered in the rhythm clubs (now defunct) and preserved by the Dixielanders was increasingly associated with modern jazz but the debates about the relative values of New Orleans jazz and be-bop were intense precisely because both sides assumed their music mattered (and despised whoever made the bestseller lists). Francis Newton's 1959 description of the typical jazz fan covers advocates of traditional and modern sounds alike:

> As a type he has always and everywhere had clearly recognisable characteristics, the first of which is his stubborn refusal to be confused with the 'pop' fan. He is passionately 'anti-commercial', to the point where the mere fact that an artist attracts the larger box-office is often regarded as *prima facie* evidence of musical treason, or even where the musician who dresses properly for his stage appearance may get black looks from the more incorruptible fans.[10]

Newton went on to suggest that 'the quintessential location of the fan is not the dance hall, the night club, or even the jazz concert or club, but the private room in which a group of young men play one another records, repeating crucial passages until they are worn out, and then endlessly discussing their comparative merits.' This was the world of the lower–middle–class, young, predominantly male, suburban, self-educated, would-be cultured, self-defined musical connoisseurs (a world still recognizable, thirty years later, as the readership of *NME*). In the 1950s such fans were probably not themselves musicians but they were quite likely to have 'artistic' career plans – art colleges provided their higher education. In the sparse statistics available of 1950s jazz fans, commercial and graphic artists show up most regularly. Jazz represented for them, in Newton's words, not 'a retreat into unintellectualism' but 'a way of achieving intellectualism the independent way'. [11]

For these fans, for art school students generally, there was still a clear distinction between art and mass culture, between the hard task-master of authentic self-expression and the easy commercial calculations involved in pleasing the public. The bohemian element of artistic life, the Romantic suggestion that a true artist couldn't be shackled by bourgeois convention or bourgeois morality, didn't yet involve any attempt to grapple with the equally restricting temptations of the mass market place. And so jazz (not rock 'n' roll), jazz as it had been defined by a generation of serious fans, became bohemian music, the soundtrack of disgust at the new 'affluent' 'admass' society (as it was, for instance, for Jimmy Porter in *Look Back in Anger*) and the sign of a cool, individual sensibility (as it was for the hero of Colin MacInnes's *Absolute Beginners*). Even when the original British Pop artists began to reassess mass culture, it was still American commercial art that concerned them, icons and styling nuances that could be used to make mock of stuffy English ways; the first signs of a new British pop culture were ignored. As George Melly puts it, 'although the ICA's theologians were conscious of the emergence of Tommy Steele and Company they were far too busy genuflecting in front of American culture to pay them any attention.' [12]

The first art school graduates to enter the British commercial world gleefully, rather than as a matter of occupational necessity, were, then, fashion designers. George Melly describes Bazaar, the clothes shop opened in 1955 on the King's Road by Mary Quant and Alexander Plunket Greene (a symbolic match of art schools' upper and lower middle classes) and by the end of the decade the source of a new High Street look as 'the one true pop manifestation in the years between [rock 'n' roll] and the Beatles', and, as Mary Quant's own autobiography makes clear, what mattered about Bazaar was not its origins (another idiosyncratic clothes shop for the rich) but its implications: it established the 'boutique' as a tool of mass marketing, meant that Quant, as designer, had to be interested in the look of the lower classes (the essence of her designs was, in her terms, their 'classlessness'). At about the same time, Janey Ironside, who became RCA Professor of Fashion in 1956, found herself dealing with students who were, by temperament and origin, more interested in popular taste than high fashion, more intrigued by youth fads than the classic look. She attributed this to the new art educational opportunities opened up by the 1944 Education Act and full employment. [13]

By the end of the 1950s, art college lecturers, or, at least, those few who made up the Pop art movement, were beginning to appropriate elements of mass culture for their own aesthetic ends, while art college graduates, or, at least, those few who made up the best fashion departments, were bringing to the mass market elements of bohemian style – the beatnik look, 'an idiomatic jazz-cellar raciness', French New Wave iconography as featured in the first fashion photographs of David Bailey, the modernist *pose*. But for the history of pop music, what mattered most about these early signs of the 'swinging sixties' was their interplay in coffee bar culture with the latest 'authentic' blues-based sounds, skiffle and r 'n' b – it was from the combination of these contrasting ideas of do-it-yourself Bohemia that the astonishing art school beat boom was to emerge. [14]

British beat and the triumph of Romanticism

Richards stood out even then in his dress and through his music. While everyone else played traditional songs like 'San Francisco Bay Blues' or 'Cocaine', he would strike a Presley chord.

'Keith was a loner and always seemed to be quiet. He was an absolute lout,' [Dick] Taylor says affectionately. 'But a really nice lout. He'd sit and play an Elvis song, "I'm Left, You're Right, She's Gone" while everyone else would be playing those nonsense folky songs. Keith really was the school rocker.' [15]

The first of Britain's art school blues musicians, John Mayall, attended junior art classes in Manchester in the 1940s, debuted as a pianist in a blues trio in 1950, and formed the first version of his Powerhouse Four when he returned to the Regional College of Art after a couple of years National Service. For the next decade (and even after his move to London and the buoyant Southern r & b scene in 1963) Mayall took commercial art and graphic layout jobs by day, blues gigs by night, and lived a life much like that of the original Dixielanders – he even had the same reputation as George Webb for 'purism' and an intimidating disapproval of band members who strayed away from the correct blues line. But while Mayall's stance was to be significant well into the 1960s (in his famous 1965 gesture of anti-commercialism, Eric Clapton left his art school band, the Yardbirds, to join John Mayall's Bluesbreakers) by then there were other ideological positions involved in art school students' attitudes to music-making.

John Lennon, who was at Liverpool College of Art from 1957-60, best exemplified the changes. For a start he was there as much for negative as positive reasons. He was a bright, disruptive, lower-class grammar school boy with no O-levels, no career plans, and nowhere else to go (and when he left the college three years later he had no art qualifications either). Lennon was, then, happy to go to art school simply because 'it was better than working' (and as an unqualified entrant, with few signs of artistic talent anyway, he found himself on a lettering course as dull as his school subjects). This was the period, from the mid-1950s to the mid-1960s, when art schools operated most liberally to provide further educational opportunities to working- and middle-class school leavers who had neither academic nor occupational qualifications but whose 'awkwardness' seemed to have some sort of creative potential. In 1959, for example, Keith Richards, council estate yob and truant, was expelled from secondary school and wangled a place at Sidcup College of Art, while Chris Dreja, later of the Yardbirds, then of the Surbiton middle class, found himself placed in his secondary mod's 'pre-art school set-up called the "art-stream" '. Dreja had failed the 11 + and already, as a thirteen-year-old, was obviously 'anti-social' but, as he remembers, 'if you took certain aptitude tests or your hair was too long and you didn't fit in anywhere else' you were defined as an art school type. Dreja joined the art stream experiment in its third year; two years above him were Eric Clapton 'plus a whole collection of other buffoons and social drop-outs'. [16]

For such misfits and rebels, art college was as much an ideological battleground as school had been, and fellow students were as despised for their sloppy bohemian pose as fellow school pupils had been for their stupidity and/or eagerness to please. Lennon and Richards alike thus played up their supposed working classness, dressing up as teddy boys (or what their peers thought were teddy boys), using rock 'n' roll as a sign of their contemptuous vulgarity.

'I think it is shit music,' John Lennon sneered about jazz, 'even more stupid than rock and roll, followed by students in Marks and Spencer pullovers. Jazz never gets anywhere, never does anything, it's always the same and all they do is drink pints of beer.' Fellow student Michael Isaacson, who ran the college music club 'and provided a staple diet of jazz, notably the trendy sounds of Miles Davis and the Modern Jazz Quartet', remembers Lennon's response: 'What a lot of fucking shit you play. Why don't you play something proper – like Little Richard, Chuck Berry, Elvis Presley?'

> Isaacson's retort was a challenge: 'What do *you* know about it? Most of the people here like this. If you really want to do something, bring your group to the art school dance and prove yourselves. I'll put you on and give you a break.' The group did play, and Isaacson says they were a shambles, with a poor sound, and deservedly got a thin reception. [17]

Even as they were being awkward and rude, taking their own musical interests far more seriously than their fellow students' artistic skills, using rock 'n' roll as a way of puncturing bohemian pomposity, students like Lennon were finding unexpected opportunities in art school life and were being changed by them. At the very least colleges offered even the idlest students material benefits. They provided stages and audiences for first, faltering performances, and while reception may have been 'thin', college audiences have always put less value on 'professionalism', been more open to experiment and surprise than any other group of rock and pop fans. Entertainment doesn't necessarily define an art school night out; bad performances can easily be transformed, by the right sort of self-

'Sloppy bohemians pose'

consciousness, into good performance art (or ordinary Dada). Take this (1980s) account of Blancmange:

> Neil and Stephen met whilst graphic students at Harrow College. Stephen was dabbling in keyboards in a jazzy workshop-type ensemble that had commandeered the college bar for an evening of avant-amusements. Neil had a part in a seven strong grouping dedicated to the destruction of old Beatle songs.

> Stephen: 'The night Neil saw us we had five percussionists and the bar was full of lawnmowers and washing machines. We used to mike those things up and they would just go.'

> Neil: 'The noise they made fitted in with what I'd been doing. Only one of my lot could actually play, we just used to go overboard in performance. We'd bring loads of equipment and borrow amps that we'd never use just so the whole thing looked bigger. We used to dream of playing the college bar. It was *the* gig.'[18]

In the late 1950s experiments were mostly less drastic (though even then John Lennon would have probably enjoyed destroying Beatle songs) but equally necessary – they gave musicians a chance to make music without having to please anyone, without having to fit either the showbiz routines which had already changed the approach of rock 'n' rollers like Cliff Richard or the rapidly hardening formulas of jazz, folk and skiffle clubs. Colleges provided rehearsal space and time – lunch sessions seem to have been routine in all art colleges, and even Jimmy Page, who arrived at art school as a well-established rock and roll guitarist, found college life valuable simply for its lack of formal demands – 'he immersed himself in blues studies, collecting old records, practising hours every day.'[19]

For less worldly, less experienced students, the most valuable college resource was other students, who provided ideas, records, equipment, moral support, even money. It was in college that Keith Richards first heard American blues, got an electric guitar (in a swop for some records), and played in an r & b band. It was from a college friend, Andy 'Thunderclap' Newman, that Pete Townshend learnt the creative use of tape recording. It was at a college gig that Ray Davies met Alexis Korner and so got access to the London r & b scene. It was thanks to his college contacts that John Lennon improved the early Beatles sound – they became the first of many groups to subsidize their equipment costs illicitly, from student union funds!

In a sense all we're describing here is a familiar aspect of student life – art colleges were special in the late 1950s and early 1960s only because universities and technical colleges then catered for a much narrower range of student interests, demanded much more systematic academic work, and weren't yet into the entertainment business. But art school friendships also involve attitudes and influences that are not normal in other educational settings even now – they offer a way for students to apply the tenets of Romanticism (all art students are, after all, in one way or another, 'creative') to everyday life. For Pete Townshend, for example, friendship with Tom Wright didn't just mean access to 'a massive collection of American blues, R & B and jazz albums'. Wright also gave Townshend 'his first taste of marijuana', and, as Dave Marsh comments:

> At the time, one of the major functions of pot smoking was to throw Townshend together with a group of very unconventional students, leading him to question the relative social stability in which he'd been raised and supporting his ego by marking him as eccentric rather than just weird.[20]

Eric Burdon remembers meeting John Steel (who became The Animals' drummer) in his very first class at Newcastle College of Art ('I heard someone yell from the back of the room: "Is anyone here interested in jazz?" ') and the two of them were soon part of the college clique who dominated lunchtime jam sessions and the studio record player, spending the rest of their time in 'frantic' record exchanging, film-going and discussions of white American beat style and black American beat music. For John Lennon, by far the most significant aspect of art school life was his friendship with students like Bill Harry and, in particular, Stuart Sutcliffe – 'they would sit for hours in Ye Cracke', the student pub, 'discussing Henry Miller and Kerouac and the "beat" poets, Corso and Ferlinghetti'. Lennon had always regarded himself as a genius; Sutcliffe taught him, by both precept and example, what it meant to be an 'artist':

From Stu, he learned of the French Impressionists, whose

rebellion against accepted values made that of Rock and Roll seem marginal. Van Gogh, even more than Elvis Presley, now became the hero against whom John Lennon measured the world. [21]

Through Sutcliffe, Lennon (and the Beatles) became, first, part of the Liverpool 8 art scene, the bohemian cafés, pubs, clubs and pads (the flat Sutcliffe and Lennon shared in Gambier Terrace was even featured in the *People* as an example of 'beatnik horror'), and, then, part of the Hamburg art scene (so that, eventually, Lennon moved from wearing a rock hairstyle to shock the art school world to wearing an art school hairstyle to shock the pop world). [22]

The changes in Liverpool music in this period weren't caused by the Beatles (or by art schools). The Cavern, which had started as a trad jazz hangout, had already moved into modern jazz and skiffle, and became a 'beat club' in 1960 out of commercial necessity (just as the jazz group the Bluegenes became a beat group, the Swinging Blue Jeans). The Beatles' importance (or, rather, the importance of Lennon and Sutcliffe) was to keep a sense of Bohemia alive in the club, even as it drew a younger, lower class, more casually hedonistic crowd, and to apply an artistic attitude to these youths' concerns for style and rock 'n' roll. Lennon had, indeed, first been drawn to Sutcliffe by the way he looked:

> For Stu, in 1959, resembled neither Teddy Boy nor Jazz cellar habitué. He had evolved his own style of skin-tight jeans, pink shirts with pinned collars and pointed boots with high, elasticated sides. His dress, in fact, was disapproved of by the Art College far more than John's, but was tolerated because of his brilliance as a student. [23]

Chris Dreja remembers that even in his pre-college art stream, fashion sense (this was in the earliest days of mod) was as significant a mark of the 'artistic' temperament as an aptitude for drawing – by 1960 the fifteen-year-old Clapton was going through 'a phase of wearing blue plastic "pacca-macs", and back-combing his hair into amazing bouffant styles.' At about the same time Keith Richards had come through his 'teddy boy period' and was wearing his own idiosyncratic version of 'art school "gear"', with denim drainpipe trousers, a jean-jacket and mauve-striped shirts'. When in 1964 manager Pete Meaden decided that the Who, an r & b band, should become the High Numbers, a mod band, Pete Townshend was much more enthusiastic than the rest of the group. He wasn't a mod – 'I was at art college, had long hair, was smoking pot and going with girls with long red hair, and all that. Painting farty pictures and carrying my portfolio around . . . I had to learn how to be a mod.' But this was, none the less, an artistic challenge: 'I was trained in graphic design . . . '

> When the band started, I used to say, 'Listen, we should look right, we should walk in a particular way, should talk in a particular way. We should look different from other people. After a concert is over, if we go to talk to people, we should maintain a facade.'[24]

Our argument about this crucial period in British pop history is not that all significant British musicians were at art school but that those who were, brought into music-making attitudes that could never have been fostered under the pressures of professional entertainment. Over the next few years the art school connection became the best explanation of why some British beat groups made a successful move into the new rock culture (in pursuit of creative challenge), while others were doomed to play out their careers in performances of their old 'entertaining' hits night after night on the working men's club and cabaret circuit. Compare, for example, the Beatles' progress with the dead ends which virtually all their Merseybeat colleagues reached, and consider the importance of their provincial art school experience for such rock stars as Eric Burdon (Newcastle and the Animals), Roy Wood (Moseley and the Move), Christine Perfect (Birmingham, Chicken Shack, Fleetwood Mac) and Charlie Whitney (Leicester and the Family). But what's most striking in this period is the domination of British rock, after the brief provincial boom, by musicians from those London suburbs where the interplay of art school and youth culture was most obvious. This interplay was partly a matter of personnel (Pete Townshend, for example, like many young London musicians in the early 1960s, was an art student by day, but a Detour or Who or High Number by night – and his fellow band members were not fellow students), and partly a matter of style – the mod cult had its own concern for visual pose and sophistication, its own roots in 1950s beatnik coffee bar culture, its own ties with the new generation of fashion students. And it was marked by a geographical confluence of interests.

Eel Pie Island, the most notorious gathering spot for London's r & b fans best exemplifies the cultural alliances involved:

> Tea-dances were held there in the twenties, but its use was sporadic until 1956, when Arthur Chisnall opened [the hotel] as a jazz club. 'The Island', as it was known, was never just a club, always something much more than that. Essentially it was set up to cater for the emerging South West London Art School crowd, not as a commercial venture but more as a radical, bohemian cultural centre. By the late fifties it was where every parent told their offspring not to go, with the result that they flocked there in droves. Although it started out as a jazz club, the Island went with the changes, and by early '63 was regularly featuring R'N'B, notable regulars being Cyril Davies' band, the All Stars.[25]

Eel Pie Island was a bohemian resource which attracted crowds of mods, and it can be argued that the whole Richmond/Kingston area, precisely because of the number of art colleges around, was 'developing a Soho of its own'. The newly affluent West London school leavers, white collar teenagers, began to spend their money in college pubs and clubs, to leave home to live in rooms in Richmond's 'student' houses. Coffee bars were the first sign of this youth movement:

> The most notorious in the area – or the best depending on your point of view – was L'Auberge, in Richmond, next to the Odeon cinema. It was opened in 1956 and was based on the famous Partisan Coffee Bar in Soho. It was open until two in the morning, had a great juke-box, and no one would hassle you if you sat all night over one coffee. It continued to operate on these lines until 1966.[26]

Richard Barnes has similar fond memories of the café opposite Ealing College, which had half the space on the juke box for students' own records and thereby attracted 'the mods from the adjoining catering and commercial colleges'.[27]

It was in these south and west London settings, even more clearly than in provincial haunts like the Cavern, that two previously separate worlds came together – the obsessive record collectors and earnest 'students' of the blues on the one hand, and youthful pleasure-seekers on the other – and it was in these settings that the new generation of art school musicians, who straddled both worlds, developed an ideology of music-making that kept both groups of fans in play together (an ideology which was duly taken up by those ambitious mods, like David Bowie and Marc Bolan, who had artistic ambitions without, in fact, going to art school).

What mattered most for these musicians was the old rhythm club idea of authenticity, which, for them, had two components – first, a concern for the origins and roots of rock and roll, a search for 'genuine' black American dance music; second, a concern for 'rawness', for a direct emotional expression to cut through the trappings of showbiz. The peculiarity of purist British blues groups imitating American records was justified (as purist British New Orleans groups had justified their cover versions) in the name of a stylistic and emotional truth. The blues was the most honest music and so blues performers must be the most honest musicians, regardless of their actual circumstances. No one seemed to doubt that this blues magic could survive its translation into a new setting – these performers believed they were made authentic *by* their sounds. In this context 'commercial' music meant lying music, pop was by its nature false. Groups like Cyril Davies's All Stars and John Mayall's Bluesbreakers and, indeed, the Rolling Stones may have been entertaining sell-out crowds each weekend but they certainly weren't 'giving the people what they want'. These bands (and their fans) were quick to distinguish themselves from such vacuous pop groups as the Dave Clark Five. As the Rolling Stones official biography argued in 1964:

Many top pop groups achieve their fame and stardom and then go out, quite deliberately, to encourage adults and parents to like them. This doesn't appeal to the forthright Stones. They will not make any conscious effort to be liked by anybody at all – not even their present fans if it also meant changing their own way of life. The Stones have been Rebels With A Cause ... the cause of rhythm 'n' blues music. [28]

As the Stones' rhetoric makes clear, coupled with the commitment to musical truth was a belief in r 'n' b as a means of individual expression – truth-to-the-blues couldn't be separated from truth-to-self. The Romantic ideology that floated round the art college cafeteria became part of the atmosphere of the blues clubs; if in Liverpool he replaced Elvis Presley as John Lennon's idol, in London Van Gogh took up his place in the blues pantheon alongside Muddy Waters and Howlin' Wolf. The mods' pill-popping hedonism could, thus, be redefined in terms of bohemian 'liberation', and it was this sense of individualism that distinguished the new blues musicians from older generation performers like Mayall and Alexis Korner – for a Clapton or a Jimmy Page, to be a blues guitarist meant not just honouring someone else, a black original, it was also a way of expressing individual needs, displaying individual, artistic, control.

It was this individualism that explains why these musicians, for all their explicit anti-commercialism, became pop stars – they were marketable as personalities, and their music, whatever its 'authentic' roots, could stand for the fantasies and desires of their own generation. Hence, too, the final paradox of British blues: the determined pursuit of an 'original' sound – the sound of rock's origins – became the source of a musical 'progression' – progression not just beyond what pop groups had done before but progression beyond the blues. 'Original' now meant something new. This notion of progress was defined, most influentially, by the formation of Cream in 1966. When the jazz group veterans Ginger Baker and Jack Bruce first joined Eric Clapton it was, it seemed, simply to help him play his brand of 'ancient and modern blues'. In practice, though, these blues forms were used to accompany art school poet Pete Brown's vaguely dadaist lyrics, and in concert the group soon became famous for its long, indulgent, personal improvisations. Cream was, in fact, one of the first British groups to use psychedelic lettering for its posters and psychedelic designs for its sleeves, to sell itself as art-rock. Eric Clapton admitted that:

> My whole musical attitude has changed. I listen to the same sounds and records but with a different ear. I'm no longer trying to play anything but like a white man. The time is overdue when people should play like they are and what colour they are. . . . It's a

lot easier to play in a blues band than in a group where you've got to play purely your own, individual ideas.[29]

Cream (alongside Jimmy Page's Led Zeppelin) defined the new ideology of rock. The group's commitment to musical truth inform-ed an 'anti-commercialism' which turned out to have a remarkable selling power. In their determination to be 'different' Cream excited audiences with the sheer energy of their individualism (the group were soon famous for the sound of clashing egos). The pursuit of creative autonomy turned out to be much like the pursuit of personal stardom (which is why these musicians had wanted to get up on stage in public in the first place). 'Commercialism' was only opposed when it interfered with the musicians' plans. When commerce helped them to be realized there were no complaints. Eric Clapton explained, for example, why Cream didn't go into the studio to make singles (Led Zeppelin didn't even release single tracks off their LPs):

Single sessions are terrible. I can't make them at all. They're just like – you go in there and the whole big problem is whether it's commercial. That is the problem. No matter what the music is like, it's got to be commercial, it's got to have a hook line, you've got to have this and that and you just fall into a very dark hole. I can't take it at all.[30]

But neither Clapton nor Page complained about the sales of their LPs.

Rock, then, unlike pop, was to be serious, progressive, truthful, and individual, a cluster of terms whose significance lay in the Romantic self-image of the 1960s art student, and it was to be huge-ly successful. There's one more point to be made about this. If, as Iain Chambers suggests, British beat was the sound of 'a male cam-araderie, formed at school, on the street corner, at art college or in a gang', then the art students fed into rock their own account of gender difference, an account with certain misogynistic tendencies (which were to be made obvious in 1970s cock rock). In part these reflected the usual bohemian rebellion against domesticity and the bourgeois family, the assertion that 'the artist' is, by 'his' nature, stifled by family life. To be anti-family is not necessarily to be anti-

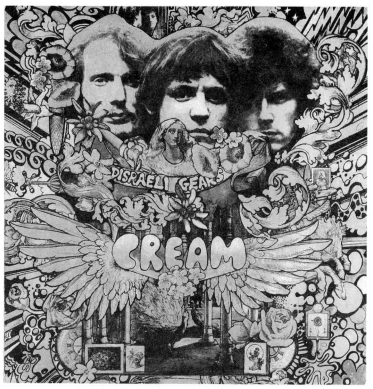

'The new ideology of rock'

woman (as feminists, and female bohemians, make clear) but as rock predominantly expressed male emotions so it took for granted (listen to Bob Dylan's early work, for example) that

> Women are the conservative and conservators, the enemies of hazard and innovation, the compromizers and temporizers. The very capacity of mothering which is their supreme gift is the greatest of all foes to masculine enterprise. [31]

These old words of H.L. Menken described the continuing attitudes of the various youth 'rebels' of the 1950s, whether Jimmy Porter and Jack Kerouac, James Dean in *Rebel Without A Cause* or Albert Finney in *Saturday Night and Sunday Morning*; they reveal how, for most young white performers the 'realism' of blues was contrasted to the 'soppiness' of teen pop in terms of a masculine versus a feminine sensibility. As the discourses of art and truth fed into popular music-making, the boundary lines between pop and rock became boundaries of gender. To take music 'seriously', from rhythm clubs to rhythm 'n' blues, was to be a man; to giggle and scream and sigh was to be a woman. As Mavis Bayton notes, even the repertoire of British blues groups was drawn from male blues – Bessie Smith songs, performed by George Melly in the 1950s, were now ignored, and Joanne Kelly's celebration of Memphis Minnie and Ida Cox remained marginal to the British blues scene. This explains, in part, why even fewer art college women became famous musicians than became famous painters, despite their equal classroom presence – there were no obvious role models, and so, as Elizabeth Wilson remembers, the 'rebellious destiny' for would-be female bohemians in the late 1950s and early 1960s was not to be a Great Artist but to be a 'Great Artist's Mistress'.[32] What's striking in rock stars' biographies is how conventionally female students (like Cynthia Lennon and Karen Astley) are defined as wives and girlfriends, how often they're situated in the one 'female' space of the college, the fashion department.

The problem for art school blues bands like the Stones and the Yardbirds was that they became pop stars anyway, and found themselves playing, for all their masculine 'seriousness', to female teenagers. The solution was to Romanticize this relationship too, to treat audiences as artists' models, subject to particular forms of sexual power and manipulation. David Bailey's relationship with Jean Shrimpton and, through her, with all those women who took her as their fashion 'model', became the rock star norm, whether literally (George Harrison was the first of many musicians to marry a model, and the press was soon fascinated by the scruffy star/bourgeois girlfriend story – McCartney and Jane Asher, Jagger and Marianne Faithfull, Clapton and Alice Ormsby Gore) or metaphorically, in the organization of performance – the Stones' relationship with their audience, for example, had an erotic charge, a sado-masochistic element, quite absent from, say, Cliff Richard's teasing relationship with his female fans. Artistic self-consciousness began to feed into *all* aspects of pop. Art school musicians, having established their 'authenticity' as music-makers, now had to deal with the sales process.

Art pop/Pop art

Q: Who would you most like to have been?
Ray Davies: I'd like to be a painter . . . I admire Rembrandt a lot. He was like a recording artist, he went from one company, if you like, one financier to another.

Q: What was the first thing, art-wise, which moved you?
Bryan Ferry: I think it was the first time I saw a really strong presentation, which was a touring production of the opera La Bohème at the Theatre Royal in Newcastle. It had quite a strong effect on me, the whole thing of bohemian life, the romantic life, the sacrifice for art. [33]

I remember Mick was in a band called Liberation. That was what bands used to call themselves. They didn't want to make money. They called it art and were in it for the psychic experience. (Pam Smitham, remembering the Coventry music scene in the late 1960s) [34]

The immediate effect of the art school takeover of beat music in the name of bohemian Romanticism was to make rock attractive to already existing Romantic bohemians. This had the most dramatic consequences in San Francisco. By the late 1950s San Francisco had the USA's most self-conscious Bohemia, a rather precious community of beat poets, white jazz musicians, semi-successful painters and sculptors, would-be creators of all sorts. These men and women were young (often surviving economically on the fringes of the Bay Area's college scene) but not much interested in rock music. Their clubs and bars featured jazz and folk; for the San Francisco beats, as for Britain's 1950s art students, it was important to distance themselves from the mainstream white popular culture of affluence, from Eisenhower complacency and the TV watching/magazine reading world of Middle America – and rock 'n' roll had long since been integrated into the conformist routines of high school culture.

And so, as John Cippollina of Quicksilver Messenger Service later remembered, for young musicians, 'it was an unwritten law: it's okay to play rock 'n' roll until you were eighteen; after that it's folk,' while most local performers didn't even play rock 'n' roll in the first place. Which meant, as Charles Perry notes, that even after the rise of the Californian Sound, 'most of the rock musicians in San Francisco were basically folkies learning how to play electrified instruments.'[35]

For these musicians British beat was both a musical and social revelation. On the one hand, British chart groups, led by the Beatles, revealed that black and white American pop could be used to make music every bit as individual and expressive as black and white American folk; on the other hand, British r & b groups, led by the Rolling Stones, revealed that it was possible to be commercially successful while keeping all one's bohemian credentials intact. It seems to have been, indeed, the Rolling Stones' show at the San Francisco Civic Auditorium on 14 May 1965, which triggered off the whole psychedelic music movement. The concert inspired Ron Nagle, a ceramics graduate from San Francisco State College, to form a band, The Terrazzo Brothers, and to put on a rock 'n' roll party, recruiting the players and most of their audience from the San Francisco Art Institute. The resulting concert was the model for all the city's later rock events:

> It was like a license to get up there and act weird. It was the art school mentality. A lot of English groups had come out of art schools just like us and the only guys around the city who had long hair then were artists too . . . [36]

Up to this moment American art schools don't seem to have produced students with much music-making interest, though also in the Stones' May audience was George Hunter, an artist who'd been studying electronic music at San Francisco State, and working with a dance troupe. For Hunter, as for Nagle, what the Beatles and now the Stones meant was that artistic ambitions could be realized in the pop media too:

> 'I was still into Happenings when I first got the idea of starting a music group,' Hunter recounts. 'What I wanted to do was build a mixing board with bell gates, ring modulators and other

synthesising devices that could mould and shape the sound of the instruments and have everybody patched into that – a massive sound system for us all to play through. It was really just all concept back then. I hadn't really worked on the direction the music was going to take.'

He was hardly, however, short on strange notions. 'I was going to call the group The Androids,' continues Hunter. 'I wanted to put together a group of men and women with identical haircuts and clothes. Sort of a unisex-android approach, early techno-pop, a combination of everything I'd been working on up to that point.'[37]

Instead, he formed the Charlatans, the first real San Francisco group, would-be Beatles in local, gold-rush Edwardian suits and mop-tops who played old r & b and rock 'n' roll songs on acid. What mattered about the Charlatans, though, wasn't their sound as such, but their *performance* – it was Hunter who first brought the idea of the Happening, a total experience, senses out of control, to the pop show. And as the San Francisco rock scene began to develop, fine artists were involved not just as musicians, but as designers, as sculptors, as *visual* experts. The light show, for example, became an integral part of San Francisco dance halls. Using a technique – light projected through moving, liquid pigments – invented by a San Francisco State art professor in 1952, visuals had long been used to accompany poetry readings, jazz drummers, experimental theatre groups and so on; now they were employed by rock groups and rock promoters, and individual artists became known for their different lighting styles. Poster artists, too, were key members of the psychedelic scene. George Hunter himself was a devotee of the turn-of-the-century illustrator Maxfield Parrish, and had used Parrish's style on the posters the Charlatans made to advertise their earliest performances. It now became the norm for both groups and concert halls to use local artists to advertise themselves, drawing particularly on the work of people like Stanley Mouse, Rick Griffin and Victor Moscoso, who were already working in 'popular' media – cartoons and comic books, custom car and bike design. Lenny Kaye suggests that what happened in San Francisco was a West Coast version of Pop art:

Pop art was founded on a populist ethic, the everyday made eternal, a depth within surface, the in-joke of the put-on and readymade. Pop art was constructed for the Now, a paper dress to be tossed aside after a single wearing, a 'look', a hit record. It's no coincidence that the Poster became an art form in the sixties, used by San Francisco dance-concert halls like the Fillmore and the Avalon to advertise the week's attractions in an optically hypnotic style . . . [38]

If British beat musicians had taken an art school sensibility into the pop world, the San Francisco musicians were part of an art world, and it was its reading of psychedelia that now fed back into the British scene. The key group here was Pink Floyd, who had begun much like any other art school band. Roger Waters was an architecture student at Regent Street Polytechnic, but bought a guitar with his grant and soon met up with the Poly's other musicians: 'in college there's always a room where people seem to gravitate with their instruments and bits of things.' Eventually, in 1965, he formed Pink Floyd with a school friend, Syd Barrett (by then at Camberwell Art School), ex-Poly student Rick Wright, and architecture classmate Nick Mason. By 1966 the group was interested in mixed media shows and had 'stopped doing twelve-bar three minute numbers, i.e. we started doing one chord going on and on and seeing how we could develop that'. [39]

Pink Floyd thus already differed from most of their fellow art school r & b groups in their interest in performance and sound experiment, in their lack of interest in blues roots and musical soulfulness. As John Walker points out:

When Pink Floyd were developing a light show integral to their performances, technical assistance was provided by Mike Leonard, a member of Hornsey College of Art's 'Light/Sound Workshop' (founded in 1962). What the Pink Floyd and the Light/Sound Workshop had in common was a strong commitment to artistic experimentation with new media. Both groups wanted to create a 360° ambience of sounds and images. [And the group eventually used the slide/oil system developed at Hornsey by 'destruction' artist Mark Boyle.] [40]

But this also meant that they were the ideal group to symbolize the developing London art/pop scene, the 'underground' movement inspired directly by US ideas. The Floyd first came to public attention playing one of the Marquee's 'Spontaneous Underground' events, organized on Sunday afternoons by American Steve Stollman as a showcase for avant-garde writers, musicians and dancers. They were seen by Pete Jenner who was involved with the London Free School and a friend of Miles (who had started his first magazine, *Tree*, while at Cheltenham Art School in 1959) and John Hopkins, who with Miles was soon to start *International Times* (in October 1966) and the UFO Club (in December 1966). Jenner and Hopkins had already realized the financial significance of benefit concerts for London's underground institutions, and Jenner had a fantasy of signing up a successful pop group, an income source for everything else (he and Hopkins had made an unsuccessful telephone bid to manage Velvet Underground after hearing an early tape of their live show). Pink Floyd were, then, just what was required – an avant-garde beat group! – and Jenner signed them to his new management company, Blackhill Enterprises, and made them the musical leaders of the London underground (alongside the more obviously jazz based Soft Machine, who had emerged from the Canterbury art scene).[41]

For a while – quite a short while, UFO closed in October 1967 – Britain had a flourishing, London-based psychedelic movement. But for all the happenings and posters, the influence of *IT* and *OZ* (and the Australian artistic input), it was never based on a *community* of artists as in San Francisco, and soon split into different pop and rock tendencies. For Pete Jenner and his art world friends, Pink Floyd were a pop group, an accessible (and money-making) contrast to the intense intellectual sounds of avant-garde jazz and art music. But despite the success of early singles like 'See Emily Play', Pink Floyd were themselves essentially anti-pop, quickly bored with the problems of attracting a teenage audience, uninterested in the TV/radio/press paraphernalia that was necessary for hit-making. And just as other psychedelically influenced art school bands pushed up against the formal frontiers of blues (like Cream) or folk (like Fairport Convention), Pink Floyd were soon rejecting the formal constraints of pop and developing the styles of compositional complexity that were to be defined as 'progressive rock'. Like Soft Machine, they moved into LP suites, began to play concert halls to audiences as hushed as if they were at a classical event. For both groups their earliest records – three-minute singles, debut LPs of 'weird' but catchy tunes – seem anomalous, and for Floyd the move away from pop was marked by parting company with Syd Barrett, who'd written their best songs, and Blackhill.

One of Pete Jenner's last schemes for them was an Arts Council grant to support a tour. His application was unsuccessful (though, later, both Soft Machine and Henry Cow did get assistance – 'progressive' rock was acknowledged as having artistic merit) but its implication was, indeed, that the Floyd were not really a 'popular' group. In fact progressive (or art) rock was to become the most commercially successful British sound of all in the early 1970s, with Pink Floyd's *Dark Side of the Moon* one of the bestselling LPs ever. The group had resolved the tension they'd originally felt between artistic and commercial logic by asserting complete artistic control and becoming astonishingly rich anyway! They seemed to achieve the 1960s art school ideal – expressing an individual vision of the world, using every technological resource available to them, uncorrupted by the pop process, making a good living. They benefited even more than Cream from the diffusion of Romantic ideology among the rock audience. The Floyd's fans were equally determined to be different from ordinary pop people and they realised this through superior *consumption*.

The importance of the psychedelic movement was that in bringing the worlds of art and pop together it focused a question that had only vaguely worried the original art school musicians: what did it mean to be an 'artist' in a mass medium? For progressive musicians like the Floyd the answer was clear. Artistic status depended on personal autonomy, on the ability to use mass media forms without being used by them; there was a clear difference between rock music – which might reach a mass public via mass media but was made according to the artistic choices of its creators – and pop music, which was determined in both form and content by market considerations. Art rock – a musical form claimed in the name of Romantic tradition – was thus different from art pop, music made according to an aesthetic of the everyday and the disposable, and while Lenny

Kaye might be right to claim San Francisco posters as Pop art, in general the US psychedelic scene remained as old-fashioned in its artistic self-consciousness as the British art rockers. Even in California the real Pop art scene in the sixties was not the Bay Area but Los Angeles, which had almost as significant a youth music market (one noticeably influenced by the British mod movement) and a much more flippant, dilettante artistic community. The presence of the film and television industry seemed to make everyone aware of the importance of appearances:

> 'There's a difference between freaks and hippies,' Frank Zappa said, defending L.A. to *Rolling Stone* in 1968. 'Hippies don't really care what they look like and the freaks care an awful lot. Their packaging and image construction is a very important part of their lifestyle.'[42]

For musicians like Zappa, the challenge was to be bohemian within the pop process. Commercialism was *always* the issue – the satirical target of early Mothers of Invention LPs like *We're Only In It For the Money* with its parody of the *Sgt Pepper* cover (the Beatles were not amused). Market forces could not be ignored, as they often seemed to be by the San Francisco musicians, who fantasized about being true stars but did little to achieve their ambition – it took an LA event, the Monterey Jazz and Pop Festival, regarded with hostility and suspicion in the Bay Area, to translate psychedelia into big business. And in this interplay of art and commerce the important theoretical approaches were being developed elsewhere, in London and New York.

In one of the most acute attempts to make sense of British pop at the end of the 1960s, Jeff Nuttall commented that:

> The members of The Move and The Who, of The Pretty Things and The Rolling Stones, were vastly different, socially and psychologically, from the hard-case rock'n'rollers. Ex-art students, many of them, who came into pop by way of R&B, they had memories of anti-bomb protests, of the Alberts and The Temperance Seven. They knew about modern painting and sculpture, indeed their counterparts were already creating the current school of English sculpture, smooth, mechanistic, brightly coloured and

kinky, so they consequently enjoyed an appreciation of the modern movement as a whole. They broke away from traditional twelve, sixteen and thirty-two bar patterns. They composed their own increasingly sophisticated and imaginative lyrics. They increasingly ignored the mistaken dictats of managers and promoters. They introduced wild fashions that obviously owed a lot to the art school fancy dress rave. They, with their fashion designer parallels, also from the art schools, took popular culture by the scruff and whipped it far ahead of the square administration . . . Fashion then, became an applied art. As much inventiveness and creativity was employed there as in the action paintings, the collages and assemblages. [43]

What seems clearer in retrospect, though, is a distinction between the first wave of art school musicians, the London provincial r & b players who simply picked up the bohemian *attitude* and carried it with them into progressive rock, and a second generation, who applied art *theories* to pop music making (this may be the best way too to distinguish 'authentic' and 'artificial' concerns). The first star to learn more in the classroom than the coffee bar was probably Pete Townshend. He himself explained the Who's destruction of their instruments, for a while part of their performing routine, by reference to 'auto-destructive' art – Gustav Metzger had been a guest lecturer at Ealing, said Townshend, and destroyed a bass guitar as part of his talk. This was, in fact, rather a dubious example of Metzger's influence (though he was interested in the role of violence in art) and Townshend's use of the term 'auto-destructive' seems to have been the post-hoc justification of a spontaneous act. Metzger's real concern was the necessary relationship between creation and destruction (he painted in acid for example, so that his pictures were consumed even as they were made), and his influence on Townshend is more apparent in the Who's use of feedback, when the very discovery of new noise always carried with it the threat (which the group couldn't control) of the destruction of the PA system.

Metzger apparently enjoyed the Who's concerts and agreed with Townshend that pop music was as suitable a context for experiment as any other medium. Townshend himself, thanks to the enterprising policy of his course tutor, Roy Ascott, had had lecturers from the avant-garde ends of theatre, poetry and film and saw his own musical activities in terms of performance art, which meant seeing the Who's stage act itself as the moment of artistic creation and exploring the constraints on this – the dynamic relationship between star and audience, the effects of chance and accident, the shifting borders between music and noise; if nothing else, Townshend was a remarkably self-conscious pop performer, unusually able to articulate what his shows were about. And he was obviously influenced too by another strand of his art course, the Pop art theory which denied an aesthetic separation between high and mass art. Again, there was an obvious Pop art influence on the Who: Peter Blake had a role in the *look* of the group, their use of badges, medals, military memorabilia, targets and flags. Kit Lambert, the Who's manager, labelled the group 'the first pop art band', while Townshend told *Melody Maker*, 'We stand for pop art clothes, pop art music and pop art behaviour . . . we don't change offstage; we live pop art.'[44]

The importance of Townshend's use of Pop art rhetoric (and what distinguished him from the r & b bohemians) was that it referred not to music-making as such – to the issue of self-expression – but to commercial music-making, to issues of packaging, selling and publicizing, to the problems of popularity and stardom. The pioneer of an 'artistic' approach to marketing had been Andrew Loog Oldham, the Rolling Stones' manager. Oldham's first job on leaving school in 1960 was as Mary Quant's 'assistant cum window dresser cum everything else' at Bazaar, and he'd drifted through a variety of jobs in pop promotion and PR. In taking on the Stones his task, like Brian Epstein's with the Beatles, was to make a group that defined itself in opposition to the pop process, commercially successful despite itself. Oldham had little interest in the Stones' 'authenticity'. When he first saw them they were playing seated on a ring of bar stools to prove their purism: 'There was no production', Oldham says. 'It was just a Blues roots thing . . . "Here I am and this is what I'm playing." Even so, I knew what I was looking at. It was Sex.'[45] Oldham proceeded to groom his boys, put them in suits for the teen TV shows, feed titillating stories to the national press. In some respects his strategy only differed from Epstein's because of the different market profile necessary – the Beatles had been sold as good guys, the Stones would therefore be the bad guys, 'synonymous with surliness, squalor, rebellion and menace'. And Oldham had enough experience in pop PR to know how to package 'rebellious-ness' for mass youth consumption:

> To the fans, they were presented in the mode of Elvis Presley a decade previously – as rebels who were nice boys when you got to know them. No less an authority than Jimmy Savile confided to his pop column audience in *The People* newspaper that 'they're a great team for having a laugh, and dress very clean and smart when they relax.' Oldham ensured that they did everything that pop fans expected, posing as lurid colour pin-ups for teen magazines like *Rave* and *Fabulous 208*, grouped in uniform leather waistcoats or jumping up together in zany Beatle style.[46]

Epstein and Oldham, then, made exactly the same 'compromises' with the pop process (even if John Lennon was to resent the fact that the Stones, not the Beatles, got to act out rebellion). Where they differed was in how they presented what they were doing (and their own roles in doing it). For the self-effacing Epstein the point of the sales pitch was that no one should notice it being made – the Beatles just *were* the zany foursome they were sold to be. For the youthful Oldham, by contrast, just as determined to be a star as the Stones themselves, the packaging of the Stones was an art – his art – to be celebrated for its cunning and cleverness. The Stones, unlike the Beatles, remained 'authentic' artists not because their music was more rootsy nor because their image was more rebellious but because they were clearly in charge of their own selling-out process: not only did Oldham write the headlines himself – 'Would You Let Your Daughter Go With A Rolling Stone?' – but it was obvious that he did. While the Beatles had become superstars as part of a press love-in, the Stones rode to fame in a series of gleeful *games* with the media (and were, indeed, a much more camp act than the Beatles – it is difficult, in retrospect, to understand why anybody took Mick Jagger's sexuality seriously).

The Stones were, then, the first pop group to draw attention to the peculiarities of the pop process itself, leaving a wake of discomfited deejays, TV producers and journalists behind them, and Oldham was the first manager to bring sophisticated advertising ideas to their imagery. He used David Bailey, for example, (a friend from Bazaar days) to take the photos for their first LP, using no other identifying information (to Decca's dismay). Bailey's photos carried all the messages necessary in themselves – partly by 'secret' reference to Robert Freeman's cover for *With the Beatles* (the Stones looked noticeably scruffy and 'real' by contrast), partly through a use of close-up composition and half lighting that made the group look at once both near and out of reach, decadent and vulnerable.

For both mods and bohemians the Beatles were, by 1965, too clearly a part of media show-biz to be interesting. The Oldham-directed Stones, by contrast, suggested a *style* of success that though just as dependent on commercial calculation and teen appeal, had an artistic validity – the Stones could be taken (as Pete Townshend took them) as a gratifyingly successful example of Pop art.

The term 'Pop art' was first coined to describe the aesthetic value of mass-produced goods. Richard Hamilton's famous 1957 definition was, therefore, directly applicable to the contemporary phenomenon of rock 'n' roll (and Elvis Presley was an early Pop art icon). Pop art, Hamilton wrote, is

Popular (designed for a mass audience)
Transient (short-term solution)
Expendable (easily forgotten)
Low cost
Mass-produced
Young (aimed at youth)
Witty
Sexy
Gimmicky
Glamorous
Big Business[47]

For Hamilton (as we showed in chapter 1) what was under discussion was the aesthetic criterion used in the design of domestic goods. He was interested in 'art manufactured for a mass audience' in terms of the technical problems it set; he was trying to relate the solutions American mass producers had reached to design theories used by fine artists (and one question he raised, therefore, was the 'sincerity' of Pop art – 'it is not a characteristic of all but it is of some – at least, a pseudo-sincerity is'). For other members of the Independent Group of artists and critics who met in the ICA in the early 1950s the term

Pop art drew attention to the aesthetic values involved in mass consumption. The term Pop art was, for Lawrence Alloway, a way of 'expanding' conventional aesthetic discussion. Artists (and art critics) were being encouraged to take pleasure in the shapes and textures and visual devices of their everyday environment:

> The area of contact was mass-produced urban culture: movies, advertising, science fiction, pop music. We felt none of the dislike of commercial culture standard among most intellectuals, but accepted it as a fact, discussed it in detail, and consumed it enthusiastically. One result of our discussions was to take Pop culture out of the realm of 'escapism', 'sheer entertainment', 'relaxation', and to treat it with the seriousness of art.[48]

From the beginning, then, the Pop art movement had two quite different implications. The first (Hamilton's stress) was to develop an aesthetic of mass production, to take seriously as artists the people involved in designing cars and furniture, producing packages and pop stars, and, in particular, to get away from inappropriate notions (inherited from the nineteenth-century art and craft movement) of 'good taste' – the Pop art ideologues deliberately celebrated 'trashy' American goods. The second implication was that fine artists too should apply the aesthetic lessons learned from a study of mass culture, using in their own work the organization of colour and shape found on the streets and the billboards, incorporating mass-produced images into their own individual statements. Differences between Pop art styles thus depended on different sorts of plunder: compare Hamilton's intellectual response to the Americanization of visual language and Peter Blake's sentimental use of the old English designs of fairground machinery and shop fronts. Even when Blake used American imagery (like rock 'n' roll stars) he absorbed them in the British world of cigarette cards, bedroom walls and seaside display.

By the 1960s 'Pop art' had lost half its original meaning and become a term applied only to the work of those fine artists who now used popular imagery, and it is therefore necessary to follow George Melly and make a distinction between 'low Pop', mass-produced cultural goods themselves, and 'high Pop', the work of painters like Hamilton and Blake. But for 1960s art students like

Pete Townshend the tenets of Pop art, learnt now both as a fine art style *and* as an approach to industrial design, had a different resonance again: they provided them with a theoretical justification for the fun of money-making. If the Pop art theorists had challenged the aesthetic boundaries between high and mass art they had, none the less, preserved the institutional boundaries – Peter Blake and the others still made individual art objects (or, at best, limited edition posters), were still part of the gallery-centred 'art world'. For Pete Townshend, by contrast, the Who were a means of destroying the high/low distinction altogether. The group was, in itself, a 'high Pop' product with 'low Pop' impact. And musicians (their ex-students), gave the high Pop artists their first real opportunities to become bestsellers too. Peter Blake and Jan Howarth designed the *Sgt Pepper* LP sleeve and Lawrence Alloway rejoiced that 'as art is reproduced in this way it becomes itself pop culture',[49] while Richard Hamilton, employed to design the double LP *The Beatles*, delighted in the opportunity to play games with art/pop/sales conventions:

> The great attraction of the job for me was in that the power of the Beatles was such they could override the usual commercial niggling. My real employers, EMI and the company design officials, were out of the running. Another consideration was the size of the edition, potentially in the region of 5,000,000.
>
> To avoid the issue of competing with the lavish design treatments of most jackets, I suggested a plain white cover so pure and reticent that it would seem to place it in the context of the most esoteric art publications. To further this ambiguity I took it more into the little press field by individually numbering each cover. The title *The Beatles* was blind, embossed in as seemingly casual a manner as possible and the numbering had almost the appearance of a hand-numbering machine. Inside the album was a give-away 'print'. Most of the design effort and expense went into this . . . I tried to think of the print as one which would reach and please a large audience, but there were some arcane touches which only the Beatles' more intimate associates were likely to smile at. Its standards are those of a small edition print pushed, with only some technical constraints, to an edition of millions.[50]

Blake and Hamilton got their LP commssions through their agent, Robert Fraser, gallery owner and friend of the stars. The 'Swinging London' scene, even more clearly than the underground movement (though the two worlds obviously overlapped) marked a social commingling of high and low pop worlds. Gallery openings became, for a while, mass media events, celebrity gatherings (where John met Yoko). In magazines like *Queen* and the new *Sunday Times Colour Supplement* fashion photographs, pop profiles and fine art spreads were hard to distinguishy from each other, as David Bailey photographed David Hockney as if he were a pin-up. This dissolution of high Pop/low Pop boundaries was the essential visual sign of the supposed classlessness of the new Britain. The new 'artists' became famous for their upward mobility (Lennon, Bailey, Hockney). The dominant sound of gallery opening and publishing party became faked, Jagger-style cockney.

However brittle this scene (and the comic-strip, colour-montage *flair* of Swinging London took shape in the design studios of British and American advertisers and fashion magazines long before it was marketed in Carnaby Street and the King's Road) it had immense attraction to art students, who in terms of both age and training were 'experts' in low Pop/high Pop relations. They now saw 'glamorous' careers opening to them that were infinitely preferable to teaching, to the scuffle of the provincial painter. Music-making had already been established by the r & b groups as a suitable career for an art graduate – especially given what else was available[51] – and making hit records offered a particularly satisfying solution to the problem of being a Pop artist. As George Melly remarks:

the dilemma in the creation of a true pop style, a graphic equivalent of pop music, lay in the uniqueness of the art object. Whereas a record was sold cheaply in great quantities, a work of art, even a lithograph or etching, was expensive. It was partially for this reason no doubt that so many pop-minded students dropped out into pop music or preferred to move into a mass-produced area like fashion or design. There were perhaps other less ethical reasons too: the cult of instant success or bust, the belief that if you didn't make it straight from art school to a fashionable gallery you might as well give up, certainly influenced a lot of promising students; but on the credit side it was understood that in honesty the creation of objects for the pleasure of the informed few was the direct antithesis of the pop belief in art for everybody. [52]

But what matters is not that art school graduates were attracted to the pop world in the first place, but the effect their aesthetic training then had on the music they made. The art school blues bands had inherited only the Romantic notion of authenticity; for the Pop art bands what was at issue was artifice, what it meant to be an artist in an age dominated, visually, by advertising. For them pop was, in Dick Hebdige's words, 'a discourse on fashion, consumption and fine art'; a response to what Lawrence Alloway had called in 1959, 'the drama of possessions'. [53]

The first consequence of this was the increasing use of music along the lines of one of Alloway's definitions of Pop, as 'art about signs and sign systems'. Musicians (using opportunities opened up by the development of magnetic tape recording and multi-tracking) began to make music as bricolage, quoting from other work, incorporating 'real' sounds, recontextualizing familiar sonic symbols. The result could just be an anthropology of popular taste – both the Beatles and the Kinks, for example, put together notions of 'Britishness' like Peter Blake's – but for the more theoretically minded Townshend it meant making records about mass communication, about the media disruption of commonsense distinctions between the real and the false. Long before discourse theory was the norm in challenging naturalist accounts of sexuality, Pete Townshend wrote 'I'm a boy'; long before Sigue Sigue Sputnik joked about selling advertising space between their LP tracks, Townshend had masterminded *The Who Sell Out*, perhaps the Pop art pop masterpiece, the Who providing their own commercial radio context in a blend of 'true' and 'fake' jingles. What Townshend was doing here, in a strategy echoed by other Pop art influenced bands like Roy Wood's Move, and, later, Kevin Godley and Lol Creme's 10cc, was using the vitality of commerce itself, the bombardment of sales patter, to both heighten the 'realism' of the Who's music and draw attention to its spuriousness.

Pop art pop thus celebrated its own sales process (just as Oldham had done with the Stones) but in doing so set the musicians involved a problem. In entering the commercial world, in enjoying the market manipulations involved, how could they preserve their sense of artistic difference? For a while the rock 'n' roll/youth/sex/rebellion nexus seemed to be enough, in itself, to guarantee some sort of subversive status (and Townshend certainly used his fantasy youth audience like this – he defined 'the mods', an audience which in reality didn't exist, as the people who would both get his semiotic jokes and bring a critical consciousness to the sales patter) but as pop (and Pop) art was absorbed into marketing routines its 'subversiveness' seemed increasingly dubious.

By the end of the 1960s LP sleeve designers were roaming across the history of modern art, film and fashion as knowingly (and for much the same reason) as advertising agencies – the sleeves, like the rock posters and group images, at first glimpse the most obvious sign of a high art presence in rock, were, in fact, designed to sell the product. David Mellor comments in his analysis of David Bailey's 1960s significance that 'advertising stood over all as the prime integrative pop activity', and the creative pleasures of sign writing – Pop art as radical semiology – turned out to be the commercial exercise of sign-writing, putting the final touch to a display ad. Pop art, Dick Hebdige suggests, marked, 'the revenge of graphics on fine art', and the fine artists who went into pop soon found themselves cut off from the status rewards of 'authorship', from public acknowledgement of the creative individuality that marked their work – even their 'personality' was produced in a sales conference. If Pop art had appeared to offer a way of preserving the artistic impulse in the mass media world, it turned out to signal the end of Romanticism, to be an art without artists. Progressive rock was the bohemians' last bet and even Townshend, at last, abandoned pop for the 'high seriousness' of *Tommy*. [54]

In this context the key Pop art theorist was not Hamilton or any of the other British artists who, for all their interest in the mass market, remained its academic admirers only, but Andy Warhol. For Warhol the significant issue wasn't the relative merits of 'high' and 'low' art but the relationship between *all* art and 'commerce':

The person I got my art training from was Emile de Antonio – when I first met De, I was a commercial artist. In the sixties De became known for his films on Nixon and McCarthy, but back in the fifties he was an artists' agent. He connected artists with everything from neighbourhood movie houses to department stores and huge corporations . . .

De was the first person I know of to see commercial art as real art and real art as commercial art, and he made the whole New York art world see it that way too.[55]

One strand of Warhol's argument was that 'real' art's claim to be somehow non-commercial, to be based on aesthetic principles that transcend the market place, is bunkum – and part of Warhol's 'radical' effect was simply to draw attention to the high art market. He pointed out, for example, that 'to be successful as an artist, you have to have your work shown in a good gallery for the same reasons that, say, Dior never sold his originals from a counter in Woolworth's. It is a matter of marketing . . . '[56] And so, as he goes on to say, 'real' art is defined simply by the taste (and wealth) of the ruling class of the period. This implies not only that commercial art is just as good as 'real' art – its value simply being defined by other social groups, other patterns of expenditure but, also, that in democratic terms it is better, representing popular rather than elite taste (and so, in the 1980s Warhol became, effectively, the 'official' Reagan painter, the artist who most clearly represented free market populism). The further implications of this position are explained by Dieter Meier of the Swiss group Yello, an artist attracted to pop music precisely because 'it turned the elitist morality of art on its head, as a form where the market is dominated by the consumer.'

I think we're approaching a new Renaissance feeling in the arts, where the avant-garde as a petit bourgeois administered thing is definitely over. I couldn't stand depending on the rules of the petit bourgeois protectorate. The new aristocracy who tell artists what is good and what is bad is the people. They have a much better judgement than these pseudo-intellectual rulers of the avant-garde world.[57]

But Warhol's position is even more upsetting than Meier, still a Romantic artist at heart, suggests. Warhol not only put paid to the idea of the avant-garde – the best art in his terms is the most popular; market success (money!) is the only authentic form of aesthetic validation – he also denied the continuing relevance of *any* conventional concept of the 'artist'. As Morse Peckham argued in 1967:

> Since 1960 the American artist, who is the leader in the world of international art, has abdicated every essential attribute of the artist's role as his society, and any society, has traditionally conceived of it. Everything, that is, except making things, and that is why Warhol, with his extraordinary penetration (Is it intelligence? It is impossible to tell.) calls his studio the factory. And he makes things only to deny the validity of the artist's role and the validity of his culture's demand that he play it. He has deliberately stripped that role of all of its glamour, all of its importance, all of its quasi-religious significance. He has, in short, completely overturned the Romantic conception of the artist, as the alienated, cursed, tortured redeemer of the world. He offers comfortable art, art that imposes no challenges, demands no intellectual or even perceptual effort, refuses all questions, turns serious critical effort into a mockery of itself. It leaves nothing for the spectator to do, and nothing for the critic to do, and nothing for the public to do, except to buy it, if they are silly enough to do so, as they most assuredly are. [58]

For Warhol this move wasn't a moral or aesthetic decision but a necessary effect of the conditions of mass communication – whatever artists want to say will be trivialized by the media it must pass through, and so the only honest thing for the artist to do is trivialize everything; whatever the original 'complexity' or 'imaginativeness' or 'individuality' of a work it will be consumed as just another commodity, and so the only honest thing to do is create on a production line too. The commercialization of art has made it impossible to sustain a convincing Romantic or avant-garde role, and so the only means of artistic opposition left is to deny those roles' significance in the first place. And Warhol was astute enough to realize that even this highly intellectual idea of 'opposition' is spurious. It is the line both British and American Pop artists took in the 1950s and 1960s (it inspired the first group of Pop art pop stars) and it is doomed to failure because it depends on maintaining that sense of artistic 'difference' that mass market conditions deny – Rauschenberg's plundering of comic book imagery was soon featuring in advertisements; capitalist culture recuperates everything. For Warhol the point was not to oppose (or expose) this situation but to exploit it (and to exploit it in the narrowest sense – by making money).

In her 'fictional' autobiography of life at the Factory (only names were changed) Viva writes that 'Fred told Janet Lee she should give up painting and stick to movies because painting was a dead art and the only real artists today are the rock and roll singers', and Warhol told Glenn O'Brien that he had, indeed, thought of being a pop musician himself:

Warhol: Claes Oldenburg and Patti Oldenburg and Lucas Samaras and Jaspar Johns and I were starting a rock and roll group with people like La Monte Young, and the artist who digs holes in the desert now, Walter DeMaria.

O'Brien: What did you do?

Warhol: I was singing badly.[59]

And so he switched his attention to the Velvet Underground. The Velvets had already been playing mixed media events – providing the sound to films behind them, dancers in front – and Warhol simply extended the concept (adding lights, a discotheque) in his pursuit of a 'total environment': the Exploding Plastic Inevitable was, in Gerard Malanga's words, 'still more of an art than a rock event'. Superficially the Warhol/Velvet Underground shows resembled the psychedelic happenings in California (and emerged from the same collaboration of sound and visual artists) but their effect and the theory behind them were different. Ralph J. Gleason, the *San Francisco Chronicle's* champion of the San Francisco sound, commented that 'Andy Warhol's Plastic Inevitable, upon examination, turns out to be nothing more than a bad condensation of all the bum trips of the Trips Festival.' The worst thing about their San Francisco show, he wrote, was 'that it was noncreative and hence nonartistic'. And New York's own folk and poetry scene, the Greenwich Village Bohemia, was equally suspicious of the Factory. 'After a while,' remembers Dave Van Ronk, 'Andy Warhol began to come around to "collect" us. The minute we saw that towhead appear we'd just empty out.'[60]

The immediate cause of the disquiet set in motion by the Velvet Underground show was the 'ugliness' of their sound – John Cale, who came from the musical avant-garde, used drone, feedback and repetition to push against people's expectations of comfort and resolution, and Lou Reed's songs, particularly as sung by Nico, were flat accounts of pain and fear and lust with apparently no personal involvement (or moral response) at all – the group's aim was, indeed, to 'express uptightness and make the audience uptight'. But this wasn't just a New York response to the peace and love and 'natural' goodness of the West Coast sound; it also became a comment on the point – and pointlessness – of art in the new communicative order:

> None of the ideas being used were Andy's more than anybody else's, but it was undoubtedly his presence that gave the discordant production cohesion. It was also a marvellous extension of his work as a portrait artist for here one had a multi-dimensional living portrait operating once a night for a month. The movies were portraits of the people on stage. The people on stage were portraits of themselves. The songs The Velvets were singing were portraits of people. And the audience, who were being photographed, filmed and sung about as they watched the show, were being portrayed and becoming part of this giant exploding plastic inevitable tableau too.[61]

Rock and roll was a necessary part of Warhol's activities because of its public impact and money-making potential. As Paul Morrissey recalls, 'I had this idea that Andy could make money not only from underground films but from putting the movies in some sort of rock & roll context. Discovering The Velvets, bringing them up to the Factory and working with them was done for purely commercial reasons.'[62] But, in the event, Velvet Undergound were commercially unsuccessful, and their importance turned out to be not quite what Warhol had intended: they became the model for an avant-garde *within* rock and roll, the source of a self-conscious, intellectual, trash aesthetic.

The Velvet Underground's first impact was in the USA itself. They gave shape to a recognizable art school music scene (and to list American art school rockers is to describe a narrower and more distinctive pop sensibility than in Britain's colleges). Patti Smith studied painting at the Pratt Institute, Devo was formed by students in the art department at Kent State University (where Chrissie Hynde once studied), the Talking Heads came out of the Rhode Island School of Design, the 1970s Cleveland 'punk' scene of the Bush Tetras/Pere Ubu/Adele Bertai/James Chance/Dead Boys centred on the Cleveland Institute of Arts.

But the most significant art/pop community came together in the Mercer Arts Center in New York, where experimental artists (like Laurie Anderson) met a new generation of pop-oriented art school graduates (like Chris Stein of Blondie and Alan Vega of Suicide). The importance of the Mercer lay in the way it accounted for rock 'n' rollers' and avant-gardists' mutual interests. The Center was, in David Johansen's words, 'ten rooms in a hotel on Broadway and Mercer. There was an experimental video room, a cabaret room, a theatrical room. The experimental place, the Kitchen, started there. We (The New York Dolls) started on Tuesdays in the Oscar Wilde Room.'[63]

From the start, in terms of both its combination of activities and its emphasis on a particular sort of artificial 'outrage' (the New York Dolls' semi-drag glam costume was a crucial part of their act), the Mercer encouraged continuation of the kinds of collaboration between high and low art staged in the 1960s in the Factory. As Jerry Harrison (now of the Talking Heads) puts it, 'it started with the Velvet Underground and all of the things that were identified with Andy Warhol.'[64] This was as significant for would-be pop stars as for would-be cult artists. For Chris Stein, a high school musician in Brooklyn in the mid-1960s, to be interested in the art scene meant to be interested in the Factory, to be interested in rock was to be interested in the Velvet Undergound – the highpoint of his teenage career was opening a show for the Velvets at the Gymnasium. Even Iggy Pop, mid-Western, uncultivated trailer-camp boy, became an 'arty' rock musician, thanks to his friendship with Anne Wehrer, the dynamo at the heart of the Ann Arbor experimental theatre/music/film/Factory scene. In Andy Warhol's own words,

Anne Wehrer introduced me to Iggy Pop at a party at her house. It was after a performance of the Exploding Plastic Inevitable at the Ann Arbor Film Festival in 1966. He was just a kid in a bands, still in high school. He was Jim Osterberg then. I thought he was cute.

That's when he first met Nico and John Cale. It was the beginning of all that . . . his affair with Nico, a record produced by John Cale, a movie by François deMenile.[65]

The effect of the Velvet Undergound on a rock 'n' roll musician like Iggy was to give him a self-consciousness about what he was doing. His own personality became an art object, his every performance an art work (hence his impact on David Bowie, the role of the Stooges as the group linking 1960s hard rock bands to 1970s punk), and the musicians who drifted into the Mercer Arts Center in the early 1970s were all, in one way or another, similarly self-conscious. Even the Ramones were, in this setting, a wonderfully clever signification of stupidity, the most artificial sign yet of rock and roll truth.

Meanwhile, as John Rockwell argues,

'Serious' composers were attracted by rock & roll for several reasons. First, as in the late sixties [i.e. with Velvet Underground], there was a kinship between minimalism and structuralism on the one hand and a stripped-down, abstracted rock & roll on the other. By the mid-seventies, the SoHo gallery scene had become institutionalized, and the strictly visual arts were losing the creative impetus that had driven them in earlier decades. Performance art and rock performance offered a fresh challenge to many young artists. Rock entailed fewer technical demands than classical music and seemed less of a closed craft guild. It provided at least the possibility of self-support. Above all, it was the actual musical language that people – not 'the people' so much as fellow artists – preferred to speak.[66]

By the mid-1970s there was, then, in New York (and several other US cities) an 'art world' in which high and low activities were integrated, in which the mass media – TV, pop music, fashion, advertisement – were as significant for artistic output as the traditional galleries and concert halls. In mass marketing terms, though, the results weren't popular. Groups like the New York Dolls and the Stooges had little impact outside their cult audience, and while it might startle art critics that the self-proclaimed avant-garde should now play rock and roll, the consequence was not, as Warhol had originally argued, proof of the impossibility of art, but, rather, further evidence that 'artists' were, by definition, people who didn't understand popular taste.

It was, therefore, in Britain, where Pop art pop had been much more successfully sold in the 1960s, that Warhol's original message had the most resonance, thanks in particular to its influence on David Bowie and Bryan Ferry. Bowie's case was more straightforward. He had not, in fact, been at art college (though he worked for a while in graphics) but as a mod-turned-hippie he had been involved with the Beckenham Arts Lab, learning mime and picking up ideas about performance, and for him Warhol was simply the perfect *idea* of the artist, a role model like Van Gogh had been for Lennon.

Bowie celebrated Warhol in song and described his own work in Warhol-like terms:

> I've never explored anything to the point where it could be my life's work ... it was far more encouraging to me to find that when you are an artist you can turn your hand to anything, in any style. Once you have the tools then all the art forms are the same in the end.[67]

What really mattered as an artist, then, was not what you did but what you were, and Bowie became a blank canvas on which consumers write their dreams, a media-made icon to whom art happened.

Bryan Ferry, who did have an art education, was more systematic in his application of Pop theory to pop music. In his early lyrics for Roxy Music he used 'throwaway clichés and amusing phrases that you found in magazines or used in everyday speech – stylistic juxtapositions'. 'Virginia Plain', the group's first single, derived from a painting he'd done in 1964, a Pop landscape (Virginia Plain was a brand of cigarette): 'it's about driving down the freeway, passing cigarette ads on vast buildings.' He'd been dreaming of 'New York, Andy Warhol's studio, Baby Jane Holzer, Las Vegas casinos, Nevada, Route 66'. As he later told the French magazine *Rock 'n Folk*, he wrote in series of images rather than in discrete songs:

> This was an approach encouraged by the college I was at where the principal lecturer was Richard Hamilton, one of the leaders of

pop art in England. He worked on the imagery of Magazines: art inspired by commercial art as with Andy Warhol. I've tried to do the same thing with music...Mark Lancaster [who helped Warhol make the portraits of Marilyn Monroe] was one of my teachers. He greatly impressed me with his way of finding art in everyday things.[68]

Like Bowie, Ferry was concerned with pop *as* commercial art, with its packaging, its sales process. Between them the two stars made British 'glam rock' an art form – something, unlike the teenybop Sweet or camp Glary Glitter, to be taken seriously – and they remain the most significant influences in British pop. What they did, ironically, was redefine progressive rock, revitalizing the idea of the Romantic artist in terms of media fame. Having invented themselves as pop stars, Bowie and Ferry were made sense of in the old terms of rock creativity.

Warhol's arguments were developed in a different direction by Bowie/Ferry's sometime collaborator, Brian Eno. Eno's ideas are important not just because of his ubiquity in 1970s pop (like John Cale he produced a number of key punk and post-punk records in both London and New York), or because he's more articulate than any other musician, but also because his accounts of pop and art are rooted in an understanding of the technological issues involved.

Eno was a student at Ipswich and Winchester art schools, and at Ipswich was taught (like Pete Townshend a couple of years earlier at Ealing) by Roy Ascott, who used an interdisciplinary, 'cybernetic' approach to the problem of creativity. Eno remembers the shock of this for new students, still imbued with commonsense Romanticism:

> I guess that we were all united by one idea – that art school was the place where you would be able to express yourself, where the passionate and intuitive nature that you felt raged inside you would be set free and turned into art. As it happened, we couldn't have been more wrong. The first term at Ipswich was devoted entirely to getting rid of these silly ideas about the nobility of the artist by a process of complete and relentless disorientation. We were set projects that we could not understand, criticized on bases that we did not even recognize as relevant.[69]

This was the context in which Eno decided that music-making was a more interesting area of creativity than painting:

In the mid-1960s, music was definitely the happening art. Painting seemed extremely cumbersome, bunged up with old ideas and incapable as a medium of responding to a new feeling that was moving through the arts. This new feeling was expressed by the motto 'process not product' . . . Most of the country's art teachers found this orientation very difficult to stomach, because they had been educated in a climate that talked in terms of 'balance', harmony', 'spatial relationships', and 'colour values' – all of which are formal qualities of the object. And they were faced with a group of students who were effectively saying, 'I don't care what the painting *looks* like – it's simply a residue of this procedure that I am interested in'. But music seemed to avoid this dilemma completely – music was process, and any attempt to define a single performance of a piece as its *raison d'être* seemed automatically doomed. A music score is by definition a map of a set of behaviour patterns which will produce a result – but on another day that result might be entirely different. [70]

Eno's musical experiments were initially influenced by ideas developed in the classical avant-garde – John Cage's indeterminacy, La Monte Young's minimalism, and it was Young's pupil, John Cale, who most influenced Eno's approach to rock:

The Velvet Underground . . . used all of their instruments in the rhythm role almost and the singing is in a deliberate monotone, which is a deliberate non-surprise, so when you listen to the music your focus is shifting all the time because there's no ranking, which doesn't only reflect the internal structure of the music, but also the structure of your attention to it. It's not the extremes of strict ranking and focus, or no ranking and disorientation that interest me, but how much of each. I want the thing to have a certain amount of 'perceptual drift' where the ranking is being shuffled all the time, so at times you're not sure what you're meant to be listening to. [71]

What concerned Eno, then, was the development of a rock version of 'systems' music, in which what happens is no longer the result of an artistic decision – no longer *expresses* anyone – but reflects either chance or mechanical necessity, and the possibilities of both 'chance' music and 'necessary' music were being opened up by the development of electronic recording and programmable synthesizer technology. When Eno joined Roxy Music in 1971 he was not a musician (he couldn't read music and played no instrument) but a 'technical expert'. He had a Revox tape recorder and a VCS 3 synthesizer; his task was to 'treat' the group's music electronically, but no one, least of all himself, knew how it would sound as a result of these treatments. Even as a solo performer Eno's 'instruments' are the tape recorder and the recording studio, and he has always been more concerned with sound than 'meaning' – his lyrics, which at first echoed Lou Reed's 'perversity', were soon influenced by sound poetry, by surrealist automatic writing, by Dada acts like Kurt Schwitters' (and Eno stopped using words altogether in 1978).

Eno's object was to eliminate himself from his work, to minimize his 'degree of participation', to cleanse his art of the idea of the individual artist. His glamorous, ambiguous persona in Roxy Music was just another way to draw attention to the artifice of his situation (compare the earnest creative signs of early 1970s 'progressive' art rock groups like Yes and Genesis), and unlike Ferry, whose work remains embedded in the imagery that inspired the original Pop art theorists in the 1950s, Eno has taken his post-Roxy music to its anonymous conclusion, offering his own interpretation of Warhol's suggestion that real art is commercial art. In 1975 he persuaded Island to fund an 'experimental' label, Obscure, in the name of industrial 'research and development'. The only remaining point of the avant-garde, Eno suggested, is to discover 'what people need and how patterns of need change'. The only way to appreciate art now is for its everyday *usefulness*:

> I predict that the concept of 'muzak', once it sheds its connotations of aural garbage, might enjoy a new (and very fruitful) lease of life. Muzak, you see, has one great asset: you don't have to pay attention to it. This strikes me as a generous humility with which to imbue a piece of music. [72]

As a studio intellectual Eno was a seminal 1970s art/rock mediator in both Britain and the USA (crucial to the careers of David Bowie and Talking Heads, for example), but his arguments probably had the most resonance in the Federal Republic of Germany. He had, anyway, mutual interests with the FRG's electronic rock performers (who tended to come, like Can and Kraftwerk, from music colleges, and were, like Eno, inspired by Cage and Stockhausen) but his more general points about art also echoed the increasingly influential ideas of Joseph Beuys. In the words of German rock critic Klaus Frederking:

> In the early 70s the Düsseldorf Art College (under Beuys's direction) strayed away from the mainstream of West German art education (both ideologically and politically) and consequently attracted a lot of weirdos until the college got hopelessly overcrowded, so that the students had to find other places to develop their ideas. One place they gravitated towards was a venue called der Ratinger Hof, where they met with a number of creative A-level students who got high on the Pistols and the Damned in '77. Among them were Robert Görl and Gabi Delgado who then formed the nucleus of DAF. Gabi Delgado: 'a third of what I do, or probably even less, is concerned with music, more than a third, probably even half, is concerned with design and style . . . I am not a musician, I am a presenter, a propaganda minister.'[73]

Frederking points out that in the FRG, as in other north European countries (the Netherlands, for example), the influence of punk was mediated by art students: the editor of *Sounds*, the first German rock paper to take up the cause, was an ex-art student, and more than half of West Germany's significant new bands in the early 1980s came from Düsseldorf itself (including DAF, Fehlfarben, Mittagspause, Der Plan and die Krupps). At the same time musicians from these and other 'punk' and 'post punk' bands were also being written up in the media as key members of the 'New Savage' painting group (on which Beuys's influence was even more obvious).

Beuys himself has often been compared directly with Andy Warhol. Robert Hughes, for example, notes their shared 'talent for publicity'.

Astutely realizing that an artist who wants the attention of the mass media must have a uniform and a stereotype, and be seen as an identifiable product apart from his work, Beuys turned his grey fedora hat and fishing–jacket (which never came off in public) into a trademark as instantly recognizable as the silver hair and shades of Warhol's Factory days.[74]

Like Warhol, Beuys appeared to obliterate the usual distinctions between life and work, between high and low culture, between different media and academic disciplines (the reason why Beuys attracted so many students and came into conflict with the academic authorities was his willingness to teach anyone). He too rejected the argument that there could be some transcendent 'high' art, independent of everyday social relations, whether guaranteed by tradition, the artistic community or individual 'genius'. For Warhol this meant that nobody could be an 'artist' any more. All production is commodity production; all that's left to celebrate is the market – everyone can be famous for fifteen minutes because everyone is a potential commercial object. But this line of argument needn't have a Reaganite conclusion. John Rockwell, commenting on the 1970s New York music scene, suggests that:

> What Warhol and pop artists are trying to tell us – and what composer John Cage has been telling us all along – is that art isn't necessarily a product crafted painstakingly by some mysterious, removed artist-deity, but is whatever you, the perceiver, choose to perceive artistically. A Brillo box isn't suddenly art because Warhol puts a stacked bunch of them in a museum. But by putting them there he encourages you to make your every trip to the supermarket an artistic adventure, and in so doing he has exalted your life. Everybody's an artist if they want to be, which is really a more radically populist notion than encouraging scholarly studies of the blues. Roll over Beethoven indeed, and make room for us.[75]

'Everybody's an artist' was Beuys's slogan too. This partly reflected the way Pop art was originally interpreted in West Germany – its arrival coincided with the first post-war student movement, with the debates the New German Left was beginning to have with the Frankfurt tradition about 'commodity culture'. Pop was thus seen as radical in its exposure of the commodity character of *all* art (even the avant-garde). It was 'democratizing' in both practice (silk screen printing, for example, offered new means of visual propaganda) and theory – if aesthetics were now subordinate to the capitalist logic of advertising and industrial design then it became possible to 'expose' everyday life through aesthetic analysis. Beuys took up these ideas and added his own 'anthropological' reading of the Pop art argument. Everyone was an artist, in his terms, as producer as well as consumer; what we should be concerned with is how *all* people (all peoples) work on nature to produce something functional, something human, something new. For Beuys art was, in Hughes's words, 'any kind of being or doing', anything which was or could be ritualized.[76]

Beuys's thinking had obvious irrational, surreal, magical elements. For him commodities became art in so far as they could be invested with 'human' feeling and 'human' expression, and 'humanness' seemed to involve the play of instincts, fantasy and unsocialized desire. It was this approach which made his students both 'New Savage' painters and 'punk' musicians – DAF, for example, sought to put back 'forbidden' needs (for sex and death) in the 'dehumanizing' electro-disco formulas of Kraftwerk. Beuys was, despite himself, a traditionally Romantic figure, someone who transcended social forces. If everyone was an artist, he was a super-artist, as described in these typically gushing words from *The Face*:

> As a lecturer Beuys is magnetic; a shaman figure of modern times. His eyes look glazed, his rhetoric is spellbinding, his long arms gesticulate wildly. A personal confrontation with the man echoes encounters with other genius 'outsiders': John Lennon, Ian Curtis, Colin Wilson to name a few.[77]

Beuys's 'humility' had become a mark of his genius, just as Brian Eno's detached scientific reason became a mark of his (and he even had a boffin's dome to prove it). As Robert Hewison puts it: 'with the destruction of the art, the artist is not destroyed but elevated, and the personality of the artist becomes a substitute for the forms of the art.'[78]

Pop had started with the argument that old ideas of high art could not survive mass communications and the subordination of all culture to the power of the commodity. Those ideas were now a selling point – a trade mark – of consumer goods themselves. Eno might strive to make muzak, but his career was in fact celebrated with a deluxe box record set, a retrospective, and a plush coffee table art book (produced under the auspices of Pete Townshend at Faber & Faber, any visual, *expressive*, gaps filled solemnly by Russell Mills). Pop had made Art big business, and neither art nor pop could be the same again.

4
THE POP SITUATIONISTS

I went to art school like everybody else. I wanted to be an artist. But when I got there, phew! What a lousy set-up. It just fucked me up completely.

(Joe Strummer)[1]

Whilst punk was supposedly throbbing on the streets (though much of that had originated in art schools), the students of the late '70s were bombarded by a new awareness from a populist group of academic and style writers. Names like Judith Williamson, Rosetta Brooks, Dick Hebdige, Ros Coward and Peter York put a new politicised version of street and fashion into the hearts, minds and portfolios of a generation of students. And ultimately feminism, street cred, anarchy and the bleak optimism of autonomy and 'indy' DIY labels found their way onto the catwalks and into the record shops and magazine pages of *Blitz*, *Ritz*, *ZG*, *The Face*, and that xeroxed bible of club chic, *i-D*. Young designers from The Royal College of Art, St Martin's, Chelsea, and the London School of Fashion considered DIY stalls at Portobello, Camden, Kensington and the King's Road a sensible alternative to chain stores or the continent. Stars were born. Vivienne Westwood made punk international, and Zandra Rhodes sunctioned up in the safe end of the street, repackaged it and sold silk and safety pins to the bank accounts of Dallas, Chicago and New York.

(Kathy Myers)[2]

I don't think there are any record companies now in the real sense of the word. We're all in the fashion business. You used to be able to sell records purely on music and musicianship. Now it's packaging, media, television and video.

(Chris Blackwell)[3]

Punk rock was the ultimate art school music movement. It brought to a head fifteen years of questions about creativity in a mass medium, and tried to keep in play bohemian ideals of authenticity *and* Pop art ideals of artifice. Its failure marked the death of rock Romanticism and the rise, instead, of the 'New Romantics'. It ushered popular music into postmodernism.

At the time of its maximum publicity, 1976-7, punk was treated as a street not a college movement, an eruption from the gutters of inner-city recession (rather than bored suburbia), and so we should stress, first, that punk as a youth subculture has a different history than punk as pop style, and, second, that there were from the start influential punk ideologues (John Peel, for example) who read punk as pre-modern, as music that restated the 'truth' of fifties rock 'n' roll and sixties beat. The punk-as-art movement was always intertwined with a punk-as-pub-rock movement, but it's the former that we mean by punk here. And it's the former that matters in terms of cultural history – what was most striking at the time, in interview after interview, was how many of the self-defined 'street' punk bands cited art rock bands as their inspiration: the Velvet Underground, the Stooges, the New York Dolls and the Ramones on the one hand; David Bowie, Roxy Music and Eno on the other. Their approach, as Peter York noted, 'drew its critical theory from the visual arts', and, in consequence, punk (increasingly loosely defined) inspired more art students to seek music-making careers than even in the mid-1960s. Dave Laing's figures, for example, suggest that 'nearly a third of the punk rock musicians had been students of some kind' (rather more than in a comparative sample of 1960s beat groups) and 'most of these in fact had studied art'.[4]

The easiest way to spell out the implications of Laing's figures is to

Postmodernists

give a brief (very incomplete) indication of some colleges' input in-
tothe late 1970s pop scene:

Royal College of Art: John Foxx and Ultravox.

Hornsey: Adam Ant, Viv Albertine (The Slits), Mike Barson
          (Madness), G. Lewis and Rob Gotobed (Wire), Lester
          Square (Monochrome Set), Steve Walsh (Manicured
          Noise).

St Martin's: Glen Matlock (Sex Pistol and Rich Kid), Lora Logic
          (of X-Ray Spex), and an increasing number of fashion

and design students who by the 1980s had founded *i-D*, taken on key roles in *The Face, Just 17, Blitz*, etc. and/or become significant clothes designers (Stephen Jones, Stephen Linard), the whole scene culminating in the appearance of Sade (who had done her foundation year in Colchester).

Central: Lene Lovich and Les Chappell; Joe Strummer.

Harrow: The Models (including Marco Pirroni, later of Adam and the Ants).

Epsom: Richard Butler (Psychedelic Furs).

Northampton: Kevin Haskins and Bauhaus.

Coventry: Hazel O'Connor, Jerry Dammers, the Specials, Selecter and 2-Tone movement.

Leeds: Marc Almond and Soft Cell, Green Gartside and Scritti Politti, The Mekons scene (including the Gang of Four, students in Leeds University's art department).

Manchester: Linder, the Ludus, and friends.

Liverpool: the scene around Deaf School (the band that linked Roxy Music to 1980s Liverpool groups like Echo and the Bunnymen, Teardrop Explodes and Wah) out of which came, among others, Budgie (of the Slits and Siouxsie and the Banshees) and Paul Rutherford (later of Frankie Goes to Hollywood) who was at St Helens; Orchestral Manoeuvres in the Dark.

Edinburgh: Jo Callis (later of the Human League), Fay Fife, Eugene Reynolds and the Rezillos.

Sheffield: Richard Kirk of Cabaret Voltaire.

This is only to scratch the surface of art college musical activity in this period and we could cite other obvious art school musicians – the Clash's Paul Simonon (Byam Shaw) and Mick Jones (Hammersmith), say (who *wore* the influence of Rauschenberg, Warhol and Jackson Pollock down their trousers) – and groups (Blancmange, Fad Gadget) and connections (the Raincoats and Bodysnatchers) and scenes (Brighton, for example). There were even art school teachers who got in on the excitement – Sarah-Jane Owen, who'd lectured in fashion at Croydon, St Martin's and the Middlesex Polytechnic, now joined The Bodysnatchers (Ian Dury had made his move from teaching art to playing music with Kilburn and the High Roads at the start of the 1970s). And art schools were the settings in which the rules of punk performance were first worked out. The Sex Pistols' first two performances were for art students and the Bromley Contingent (Siouxsie, Steve Severin, Billy Idol and friends) came together when the Pistols played the local Ravenstone College of Art (Generation X's first show was, in turn, at Central). Pete Shelley and Howard Devoto first performed publicly together as the Buzzcocks for fellow textile students at the Bolton Institute of Technology. They survived three numbers (about average for all these early punk gigs) but the point was that the art school dance was available (as it had been for 1960s groups) – even the first Rock Against Racism event was organized at the RCA – and that *any* sort of performance could be justified according to some art theory (there was always *somebody* in the audience who could apply it).[5]

The most obvious consequence of this was for punk's performing conventions, in which ideas of pop spectacle met up with the anything-goes silly-and-serious experimentation of the art event. Compare, for example, the following memories:

Pete Wylie (on the one and only performance of The Mystery Girls, featuring Pete Burns and Julian Cope, supporting Sham 69 in Eric's in Liverpool in November 1977):

> I wore my mum's most flowery blouse, and a toilet seat on my back ... it was like Captain Sensible gone absolutely haywire. It was the first time any of us had appeared in public.

Zodiac Mindwarp:

> Art school was a complete piss-take. We used to have this band called Normal Love. I'd be up there in a white head-dress looking like a skinhead Lawrence of Arabia and wearing this baggy shirt covered in curry stains. The drummer would be wearing my mum's apron with stockings and suspenders and we had this other guy in a trilby, a massive pair of Y-fronts and Doc Martens – all he did was stand there eating crisps from the eye sockets of a skull.

Mike West (on the debut performance at the 100 Club's Punk Festival by Siouxsie and the Banshees):

> Suzi and Steve planned . . . a performance in true Punk spirit – an anarchic, open-ended chanting of *The Lord's Prayer* to the accompaniment of an army of non- and almost-musicians playing dumb songs like *Goldfinger* and *Twist and Shout* until the audience could take no more and revolted against them. Steve wanted it to be something like the Velvet Underground's *Sister Ray*, while Suzi intended to carry on until she was dragged from the microphone.

In the event, only two other people got up on stage with them – Sid Vicious and Marco Pirroni – and after only twenty minutes,

> Marco mistook a signal from Steve and brought the performance to a halt – much to Suzi's annoyance as the audience was still (apparently) enjoying the performance rather than yelling for the torture to stop.

Green Gartside (on the original Scritti Politti):

> In retrospect it is hard to take stock of it. I mean, going down to the Electric Ballroom and hitting empty film cans and scratching a guitar about, playing this jittering apologetic half-reggae and singing about hegemony while putting in as many discords as you could was probably doomed to failure, I suppose.[6]

Punk performances were thus informed by avant-garde arguments about shock value, multi-media, montage and deconstruction. Artists (Throbbing Gristle are the most significant example) suddenly found that they could apply their ideas in a pop club setting and get a much more *vital* reaction than they ever got in a gallery – even gobbing was a better response to an experimental show than polite applause.

For an art group like Cabaret Voltaire – electronic musicians who combined sound and music, used tape/film collages inspired by Dada, Eno, Can and Velvet Underground, and were confined, in Sheffield, to playing to people in the music department of the university – punk simply meant new playing possibilities. In Stephen Mallinder's words,

We were swept up with the momentum of the whole thing, it was very much a movement of the moment, so we utilised it for the time being. We played gigs because we were asked to play, carrying on because we fitted in somewhere. We were left to our own devices but we still fitted in.[7]

Cabaret Voltaire were initially of interest to the Sheffield punk fanzine, *Gunrubber*

Because as well as being into music we were also into fashion. We used to buy all our clothes in London, wear all the Teddy Boy gear, etc. I think the whole idea of us intrigued people; we looked rather peculiar stemming from the early Roxy Music period, and I think people thought that we must be doing something interesting because we looked so odd.[8]

This is the other obvious art school punk effect – the punk look, at least before it was frozen into the nostalgic gesture of the provincial proletariat, followed the theoretical designs of visual experts (and was thus to evolve into the New Romantic/New Pop movement). This may be one reason why punk was, from the start, a movement that took account of gender issues: fashion departments in art schools were where women had traditionally had the strongest presence and they were certainly involved in the forming definition of punk.

The original punk scenes, as they developed, with different emphases, in Leeds and Manchester, in Liverpool and Edinburgh, and in London around the Pistols, had a strong female presence – women were musicians, fanzine editors and clothes-makers, had significant roles in management and packaging – and many of the feminist bands of the late 1970s, punk or not, had art school members (Raincoats, Slits, Bodysnatchers/Belle Stars, Brite Girls, Jam Today, Mistakes). Definitions of both masculinity and femininity, images of 'pop star' and 'bohemian artist' became problematic in new ways, and theories of consumption and audience became as crucial to punk as slogans of do-it-yourself production and the assaults on the rock establishment. We'll come back to this later. First we need to go back to the beginnings of punk, to the arguments behind the Sex Pistols.

The most articulate theorists of the art punk movement weren't the musicians but their managers. Bernie Rhodes, T-shirt designer turned Clash minder, asserted that 'all artists must be businessmen' and implied that all businessmen should be artists, a theme developed by Bob Last, whose Fast Products was the first of the new independent labels to apply art theory to marketing, and Tony Wilson, whose Factory Records was named in honour of Warhol and conceived as a 'design centre', applying the Bauhaus principle of the same 'look' for all the company's goods. These conflations of do-it-yourself business with radical theories of the 'image', were, in turn, inspired by the media success of Malcolm McLaren, ex-manager (briefly) of the New York Dolls, founder/manager of the Sex Pistols, the spider at the centre of the web which binds the seventies to the eighties, links the Pistols to Siouxsie and the Banshees to Adam and the Ants to Bow Wow Wow to Boy George to Trevor Horn. For McLaren, a 1960s art student (Harrow, Croydon, Goldsmiths), and his collaborators in Glitterbest (the Pistols' management company), graphic guerilla Jamie Reid (Wimbledon and Croydon) and clothes-maker Vivienne Westwood, pop, defined as a collision between music, fashion and street action, wasn't just a source of imagery and aesthetic life, as it had been for 1960s artists, but a *medium*. In the words of McLaren's friend and fellow student, Fred Vermorel:

The Sex Pistols was a work of art. The artists: Malcom, John (Lydon/Rotten) and Jamie (albeit with many helpers and assistants, scene changers and stand-ins). It was their collective masterpiece, a work of genius . . .

The Sex Pistols reminds me of Picasso's *Guernica*. An epochal work, inextricably tangled with the fuss and politics it provoked. And beauty wrung from despair. If the Sex Pistols is a looser and more ambiguous work, which meanders into dead corners and mediocre brushwork, this is because its jagged explosion could not be frozen on canvas in a rectangular frame but was scattered through time as banner headlines, records, rumours and anecdotes, pin-ups, video and movie footage, posters, T-shirts and fashions, and (I almost forgot) live performances. Only the shock waves remain, and the debris.

The Sex Pistols masterpiece stands at the furthermost point where artists have recognised that publicity is as important and, what is more, as *malleable* a medium as their traditional paints and clay. A point where you may anticipate and plan for the fact that the media do not simply transmit or re-produce your work, but effectively repaint – remake – it.

Malcolm and Jamie exacted an artist's revenge of which Courbet himself would have been proud. For a spell, as incandescent in its way as Palmer's vision of Shoreham, they flung news values, pictures and factoids back at the media with the concentration of Pollock hurling paint into his enormous canvases.[9]

As Pop artists, McLaren, Reid and Westwood drew on two theoretical sources. First, Warhol – McLaren had avidly attended the American Pop art exhibitions in the Whitechapel Gallery in the 1960s and had been 'especially taken by Andy Warhol, Grand Master of hype, who turned Duchamp's cottage industry in irony into mass production'. Jon Savage suggests that early punk was 'nothing so much as an English version of the Factory' (the same drug, amphetamine, the same self-obsession, the same distance, the same self-defined star *noms-de-plume*), and it's revealing that art dealer Robert Fraser was quick to pick up on the gallery potential of the Sex Pistols' 'art work', reputedly tearing posters off walls to rehang in his own house, and certainly suggesting to the V & A that they invest in Reid's 'ephemera'.[10]

But punk was also designed as *subversive* Pop art, and McLaren's theory of subversion was drawn, loosely, from situationism, from situationism as mediated by the 1968 French student movement and the London-based art school-oriented political 'groupuscule', King Mob:

And now, thanks largely to the Sex Pistols, their ideas are current in rock and roll circles. For example, the Situationist concept of 'détournement', which is turning the establishment's codes, forms and values (i.e. the hit parade) against itself, or the notion of 'recuperation' whereby the establishment (i.e. record companies) absorbs criticism by patronising it, turning its negative (i.e. creative) value into positive (i.e. appreciative and celebratory) values. And, of course, every creative person is now more acutely aware of the drag of the establishment on his/her needs and insights, the pressure to direct creativity (which is, by definition, always subversive) into cosy and harmless *cul de sacs*.[11]

Previous Pop art musicians had been recuperated either as 'stars' (like Pete Townshend) or as 'artists' (Brian Eno) or as both (Bowie and Ferry); either way, they lost control of themselves. McLaren's aim was to stay sharp by burrowing into the money-making core of the pop machine, to be both blatantly commercial (and thus resist the traditional labels of art and Bohemia) and deliberately troublesome (so that the usually smooth, hidden, gears of commerce were always on noisy display). For the theory to work, McLaren needed a successful group – without it he'd have been confined, like Genesis P-Orridge and Cosey Fan Tutte (who had quite similar ideas), to the limited shock effects of the art world fringe. And, for all his glibness, the Sex Pistols' success was never guaranteed. McLaren had the 'luck', like Warhol before him, to find a group that exactly matched his plans, but the Pistols' musical impact (on which the whole scam depended) had little to do with him – it rested on the old-fashioned rock quality of a hard rhythm section, and on Johnny Rotten's charisma. It was thanks to Rotten that the Pistols had a resonance for bored British youth, who had no interest in art theories at all (and for all his way with the mass media, McLaren never did have a radical understanding of youth culture – the punk figure he eventually created for this market was the pathetic rock 'n' roll conformist, Sid Vicious).

The Great Rock 'n' Roll Swindle was the Pistols' epitaph, not their founding statement, and the true Sex Pistols story was a tale of trial and error; its excitement came from the fact that *no one* knew what was happening. In Jamie Reid's words,

> When the Pistols were vibrant and relevant was when no-one could label them. The media couldn't label them. I mean you were National Front one day, reds under the bed another, and anarchists the next. And then it became very articulated and very CONTROLLED. In retrospect, I think the week 'God Save The Queen' got to number one we should have split the band up and got out which is what Malcolm in fact wanted to do. [12]

McLaren's importance was to make pop situationism the most convincing *explanation* of the maelstrom in which the Sex Pistols found themselves – convincing not to mainstream cultural commentators (for whom 'dole queue rock' was a sufficient label) but to punk musicians themselves and to their hippest observers. Punk, McLaren-style, 'drew attention to its own construction', and all over the country cultural studies students grappling with Barthes and Derrida (many of them in art college classrooms) were aghast – here was a cultural form in which the theories all made sense! Within months of 'God Save the Queen' punk had become the most theoretical (and theorized) music ever, as groups (like the Gang of Four and Scritti Politti) rushed from their Marxist and structuralist texts to the application of those texts. Punk was no longer a problem (to be explained by sociologists and leader writers) but a solution, a solution to the continuing dilemma of Romantic art – how to be subversive in a culture of commodities.

Dave Laing argues convincingly that the best way to understand punk is in terms of the discourses it brought into play in pop, and, he suggests, 'the only discourse by which punk rock could be defined as apart from "the rock tradition" in a positive manner was that of the avant-garde.' But, as we've already noted, what was at issue here wasn't just punk use of avant-garde discourse, but also the avant-garde's use of punk, as a discourse which could challenge the usual high art constraints. In New York, for example, where the art scene had nurtured punk in the first place, 'punk' now became a necessary rhetorical term in all sorts of visual and noise experiments. As a writer in *New York Rocker* put it in 1982: 'So there's another wave upon us. Splash! It is, as the editor of this mag told me, that Downtown Sound. It's been called Noise, art rock/rock art, skronk, rock concrete, post-modern no wave, a soundtrack for the apocalypse in progress, garage-punk-funk-jazz-electronic-communist white noise.' Old aesthetic distinctions could no longer hold, and in San Francisco a number of 'art clubs' opened, 'the A-Hole, A.R.E. (Artists for Revolution in the Eighties), Club Foot, Club Generic, Jet Wave and Valencia Tool and Die. Each set about producing performance, video, film, painting and of course music events.' Such avant-garde/punk tie-ups were equally apparent in Canada, West Germany, Switzerland, Belgium, Holland and Britain, where Cabaret Voltaire and Throbbing Gristle were featured in punk packages, Mayo Thompson of Art and Language joined Pere Ubu and worked with various Rough Trade acts and Steve Beresford, 'free' musician, played with the Slits. By the mid–1980s the ICA, an 'art club', was the most important venue in London for new British pop groups, while traditionally avant-garde acts like Sonic Youth and Test Department toured the remaining punk rooms in the provinces. [13]

For these musicians the 'punk' label (which soon covered a great range of musical styles) initially promised a shock value no longer available in the art world, where anything went (i.e. got bought); the problem they faced was to sustain this effect. What quickly happened, as Laing suggests, was that punk itself divided into a vanguard and a mainstream. 'Mainstream' punks were content (like the Damned or Clash) to run through their original songs of rage and riot in the same way for the same audience time after time, and so became as firmly institutionalized as any heavy metal band. Self-consciously experimental post-punk groups, by contrast, found themselves playing only to self-consciously experimental audiences, to critics who *expected* something novel every time. They were part of the pop scene but confined to a back field, their records mentioned only in the margins of the music press, their live appearances as dependent on state-subsidized venues and festivals as those of their experimental peers in jazz and classical music. (And as Mavis Bayton pointed out to us, this split had implications for sexual politics – the punk formula bands were soon embedded in male rock routines, feminist performers like Vi Subversa and the Au Pairs had to operate in this post-punk 'experimental' space.) Tensions only arose now for those vanguard musicians who because of past triumphs still drew a mainstream response – John Lydon's shows with Public Image Limited, for example, continued to be fraught occasions. But for most musicians the very attempt to buck the industry's usual labelling system just gave their music its own label: 'experimental pop'. The problem is well explained in the 'official' Cabaret Voltaire book:

> Cabaret Voltaire used modern day 'readymades' such as the noise of the factory, the radio, T.V. and even white noise to create rhythms much as guitars or drums could do . . . With a combination of collage and cut-up techniques, they attempted to get behind a sense of strict reality, trying to re-interpret and descramble that reality. This approach alluded to the writers of the Beat

Generation, Warhol's Factory, the sixties drug culture, and Political symbolism, rather than to any of the contemporary musicians of the time. The Cabaret Voltaire of 1973 to 1976 were involved in the manipulation of sounds, and the compilation of tapes of them. The association of these sounds within the framework of contemporary music only came later. Through the presentation of these sounds at live performances, together with a number of articles in the music papers, Cabaret Voltaire began to gain a notoriety in recognised music circles, *becoming defined as a music group*. [14]

Cabaret Voltaire became part of the 'music world' rather than the 'art world' because of the responses of other people. Avant-garde discourse as such didn't prevent them from becoming part of 'rock tradition' but assigned them a particular place within it – as an 'art' group. The Cabs always had a passive attitude to their reception, but for groups whose aim was to shake up the pop process, like, say the Gang of Four or Au Pairs, the avant-garde ghetto was no better place to be in pop than anywhere else – mass popularity was a necessary condition for the effects they wanted; commercial success was the initial goal. This is where McLaren's pop situationism became most relevant. It offered a second discourse of subversion – not in terms of the relationship of artist/art object/audience, but in terms of commodity and market. From the start his radical mystique depended on his efficiency as a businessman. Mark P of *Sniffin' Glue*, who helped define the meaning of punk, commented admiringly,

> I think Malcolm's a very clever guy. I don't think he manipulated the media, but he took advantage of every little thing. Down to the finest detail. Like every detail on his T-shirt. Every T-shirt he ever done, not one word was out. Like the Sex Pistols. No matter where you look, straight down the line, everything's perfect. Even their press handouts they used to have. Every detail. And it always used to be a nice colour. Always original. Like just every-thing. You could go on forever just saying how good they were. Even when they do old songs like 'No Fun' no one puts them down for doing that, they do it so fucking well. They're so clever. Malcolm's so clever. He's a great media person. Knows how to work with things. Knows how to sell a band. [15]

This makes McLaren sound like any good pop manager and the question becomes why having an artist in charge of a group is any different from having a businessman. How is subversive business different from successful business? (And McLaren was soon to have imitators – Steve Dagger of Spandau Ballet, ex St Martin's hustler Perry Haines, Tony James of Sigue Sigue Sputnik – who had no subversive intentions at all.) As Al Clark of Virgin commented, in the Sex Pistols story 'capitalism and anarchy far from being distant relatives were actually pillow-talk partners.' And, at the end of that story, McLaren was out-'swindled' by Richard Branson: 'in Richard he came across somebody who was his equal, I mean who was just as astute, just as inventive, just as evasive, and certainly just, as tenacious.'[16]

Pop situationism turned out to be most important as a rhetorical device too. Take this ZG account of Factory Records, founded like Glitterbest under the 'influence' of Debord's Society of the Spectacle:

> In opening a factory Tony Wilson has created a vantage point through which the teenage consumer can gain access to the apparatus and machinery whereby his [sic] own subculture/life style is manufactured. Through this access, workers/consumers at the factory gain control over the apparatus of production, and ultimately over their own role/relationship with it, gaining (albeit in some small way) 'direct possession over every moment of their activity'.

How is this effect achieved?

> Each Factory product, from its conception through to its final packaging and marketing, is treated as a product in its own right. In terms of packaging, each product is embellished with its own apparent individual identity as an art'y'fact, and yet it simultaneously contradicts this appearance by bearing upon it the unmistakeable marks of its own mass production whether it sometimes might be simply its identifying catalogue number, i.e. Fac-1, Fac-2, etc., at others a more elaborate presentation . . .
>
> The artyfact to be consumed presents the consumer with a dilemma; object'd'art [sic] or mass produced commodity? How is one to consume it? How, for example, does one approach an

album (the Durutti Column LP) of quiet melodic almost 'folkish' guitar music gently blended with synthesised rhythms, which is packaged in a sleeve of coarse sandpaper, inverting the usual package-commodity relationship whilst simultaneously threatening to destroy its rivals in the market, i.e. the consumer's record collection? . . .

. . . Each Factory product is in some way attempting to shake the consumers' 'passive' relationship with the object of consumption by creating a situation within the actual moment of consumption in which the consumer comes to question the nature of the product itself; and through this initial 'awakening' to eventually question his [sic] place within the cycles of consumption/production work/leisure, that form his everyday life in the spectacular world. [17]

This is as lucid a statement of pop situationism as can be made, but it reveals a difference between punk and post-punk versions of pop 'subversion'. McLaren and Reid, educated in the 1960s politics of art, worked in terms of spectacle and communications; in the end their King Mob tactic was to drop a brick in the cesspool of the British mass media and see what emerged. For Factory the key to the politics of the pop process is the 'moment of consumption' – the shock effect has to be built into the circulation of commodities itself. This became the recurring argument of the radical pop acts of the early 1980s, from Sheffield's ABC and Human League/Heaven 17 (making their move from avant-garde fringe to *Smash Hits* mainstream) to ZTT, and whatever its validity (Factory, for example, has been a record company much like any other, if with better graphics and a sharper grasp of the money to be made from selling records as limited edition art works) it depends for its critical promise on a theory of the market not the media. The 'sincerity' or 'authenticity' of the artist is no longer the issue. Art can only realize itself as a commodity and its meaning can only be challenged as it is consumed – all the radical cultural worker can do is seek to explode that moment.

This is where the third strand of the Glitterbest argument became important – punk as fashion. Laing suggests that

There was an ambivalence at the heart of the punk look which was often not recognised by those keen to point out the subversive potential of punk. For the punk look was also to some degree formed in relation to the existing discourse of fashion, the centre of whose power was its ability to reduce anything visual to a stylistic novelty.[18]

For McLaren and Vivienne Westwood, rag trade professionals, 'stylistic novelty' was to be another source of punk's radical effect. The point of the punk look, like that of Westwood and McLaren's previous 'subcultural' clothes (they'd begun by rethinking Teddy Boy dress), was to draw attention to the way in which fashion, in its use of the novelty/conformity axis, works as sign language. Westwood's shops – Let It Rock, which became Sex, which became Seditionaries – were never meant to service youth groups, and neither she nor McLaren had much interest in street culture as such (Westwood later told *i-D* that 'the only true example of Street Fashion that I can think of is that Rocker look').[19] Their concern, rather, was the *interplay* of producer and consumer in the making of a 'look', the way in which people both follow fashion and (mis)appropriate it. Sex, the shop, was, in fact, their original Pop art work, fashion their first canvas. They used 'low Pop' design objects and styles, plundering youth culture, gay dress codes, bondage gear, the making-do outfits of the poor and chain store taste to make 'high Pop' statements (and then 'invented' the Sex Pistols to feed their confusing images back onto the streets).

McLaren never thought much of punk as a community work and had little sympathy with the hippie/political punk patrons like Caroline Coon and John Peel, Rough Trade Records and Rock Against Racism. His radical reading of the punk look came from an argument about style; and its origins lay in design studios not unemployment lines. Writing in October 1976, as punk was becoming a media event, Peter York described a group of people he called Them, 'people who will make the supreme sacrifice: to look interesting rather than sexy'. Thems, he explained 'are excessively literate in the language of style'; their clothes are meant to be 'original or allusive or clever or witty to [their] *peers*'.[20]

York explained Thems by reference to the art school bulge of the

You're gonna wake up one morning and <u>know</u> what side of the bed you've been lying on!

(Hates:) Television (not the group)/Mick Jagger/ The Liberal Party/John Betjeman/George Melly Kenny & Cash/ Michael Caine/Charles Forte/Sat nights in Oxford Street/SECURICOR impotence or complacency (slogan & Robert Carr)/Parking tickets/19, Honey, Harpers, Vogue in fact all magazines that treat their readers as idiots/Bryan Ferry/Salvador Dali/A Touch of Class/BRUT for — who cares?/The Presidents Men/Lord Carrington/The Playboy Club/Alan Brien, Anthony Haden-Guest, Vic Lownes, to be avoided first thing in the morning/ANTIQUARIUS and all it stands for/Michael Roberts/POP STARS who are thick and useless/YES/Leo Sayer/David Essex/Top Of The Pops/Rod Stewart oh for money and an audience/Elton John — quote in NME 25 Sept re birthday spending/West End shopping/ Stirling Cooper, Jean Junction, BROWNS, Take Six, C&A/Mars bars/ Good Fun Entertainment when it's really not good or not funny Bernard Delfont/a passive audience/arse lickers/John Osborne Harry Pinter Max Bygraves Melvyn Bragg Philip Jenkinson the ICA and its symposiums John Schlesinger André Previn David Frost Peter Bogdanovich/Capital Radio/The Village Trousershop (sorry bookshop)/The narrow monopoly of media causing harmless creativity to appear subversive/THE ARTS COUNCIL/Head of the Metropolitan Police/Synthetic foods/Tate & Lyle/Corrupt councillors/ G.K.N./Grey skies/Dirty books that aren't all that dirty/Andy Warhol/ Nigel Waymouth David Hockney & Victorianism/The Stock Exchange/ Ossie Clark/The Rag Trade/E.L.P./Antiques of any sort/Housing Trusts who profit by bad housing/Bianca Jagger/Fellini/John Dunbar/J. Artur's/Tramps/Dingwalls without H/Busby Berkeley MOVIES/Sir Keith Joseph and his sensational speeches/National Front/W.H. Smith/Censorship/Chris Welch and his lost Melody Makers/Clockwork soul routines/Bob Harris (or the Sniffling Whistler as we know him)/ The job you hate but are too scared to pack in/Interview magazine — Peter Lester/rich boys dressed as poor boys/Chelita Secunda, Nicky Weymouth, June Bolan, Pauline Fordham halitosis/Rose & Anne Lambton Chinless people/Antonia Frazer/Derek Marlow/Anne Scott-James/Sydney Edwards/Christopher Logue/Osbert Lancaster/Shaw Taylor — whispering grass/The Archers/BIBAS/Old clothes old ideas and all this resting in the country business/The suburbs/The Divine Light Mission/All those fucking saints.

'Them-speak' (text of Sex T-shirt, 1976)

(Loves:) Eddie Cochran/Christine Keeler/Susan 602 2509/My monster in black tights/Raw Power/Society For Cutting Up Men/RUBBER Robin Hood Ronnie Biggs BRAZIL/Jamaican Rude Boys/Bamboo Records/ Coffee bars that sell whisky under the counter/THE SCENE – Ham Yard/Point Blank/Monica the girl who stole those paintings/Legal Aid – when you can get it/Pat Arrowsmith/Valerie Solanis/The Price Sisters/Mervin Jones article The Challenge To Capitalism in New Statesman 4th Oct. 74/Buenoventura Durutti The Black Hand Gang/ Archie Shepp Muhammed Ali Bob Marley Jimi Hendrix Sam Cooke/ Kutie Jones and his SEX PISTOLS/This country is run by a group of fascists so said Gene Vincent in a 1955 US radio interview/Seven Days with Alexander Cockburn/Olympia Press/Strange Death of Liberal England – Dangerfield/Mrs Scully love goddess from Shepherds Bush her house slaves and Search magazine/Labour Exchanges as your local/FREE RADIO stations/A chance to do it for more than a month without being ripped off/The Anarchist Spray Ballet/Lenny Bruce/Joe Orton/Ed Albee/Paustovsky/Iggy Pop/John Coltrane/Spunky James Brown/Dewey Redman/KING TUBBY'S sound system/Zoot suits and dreadlocks/Kilburn & the High Roads/Four Aces Dalston/Limbo 90 – Wolfe/Tiger Tiger – Bester/Bizarre Humphries/Woolf – Waves/Walt Whitman poet/Exupery, Simone de Beauvoir, Dashiell Hammett, Dave Cooper, Nick Kent, Carl Gayle writers/Mel Ramos painter/David Holmes the newsman/Mal Dean cartoonist/Guy Stevens records/Mal Huff funny stories/D.H./Valve amps/Art Prince/Marianne Faithfull/Jim Morrison/Alex Trocchi – Young Adam/Patrick Heron v. The Tate Gallery and all those American businesslike painters/Lady Sinthia 908 5569/Experiment with Time – Dunne/John Lacey and his boiled book v. St Martin's Art School experiment to be seen in New York. Imagination. . . .

early 1960s-70s and the resulting increase in the numbers (and status) of graduates in the applied arts of fashion and design; to the influence of Pop art, its use of images at one remove, its celebration of sleeze; and to the increasing appeal of camp, its game-playing with taste hierarchies and sexual codes. Thems had developed fashion (and design generally) in terms of pastiche, collage, self-reference, and a *confusion* of the usual rules of consistency and good taste (their approach was the counterpoint to Habitat). York suggested that David Bowie and Bryan Ferry were musical Thems, and noted that 'a group who take a dim view of much Themness are the people who run the Sex clothing store at the World's End,' but, as he then made clear, Sex and its ideology only made sense with reference to Them-speak. The Sex Pistols were a walking aesthetic critique of what everyone else was wearing; they rewrote the Romantic gesture of refusal in the terms of mass fashion (and at the high social Them event of the year, the launch party for Andy Warhol's *From A to B and Back Again*, the Sex people scrabbled for attention with Bianca Jagger).

Four years later, 'at the Blitz wine bar in Covent Garden, one of Steve Strange's and Rusty Egan's weekly "Heroes Nights" is in full swing.' Dave Rimmer describes the scene – 'punk and art students and soul boys and tranvestites and freelance oddballs all dressed, not necessarily to kill, but definitely to be noticed.' In attendance are 'a clique of Thems' (Andrew Logan, Duggie Fields), 'some characters from the artier end of punk' (Siouxsie, Billy Idol), the North London soul scene (soon to be Spandau Ballet), and 'the crowd from the Warren Street squat' (George O'Dowd, Marilyn, Andy Polaris, Jeremy Healey, Martin Degville, and their cronies from St Martin's and the Middlesex Polytechnic Art department). Rosetta Brooks, discussing 'Blitz Culture' in the first issue of her magazine, *ZG*, wrote that it was organized around the art of posing, and that

> posing can be seen as the 'ne plus ultra' of performance art. As street theatre ultimately extended into continuous performance it can be viewed as a sort of post-punk embodiment of Gilbert and George in one person (the individualist). Removed even from the hallowed context of art, the poser is his/her own ready made art object but one whose circulation is not the microcosm of the art

The art of posing

world but the self-consciously constituted clique centred upon (for the moment) the Blitz and Hell. . . . For the poser it is not so much the style of appearance which in itself is important e.g. achieving a perfect '50s revival 'look', but that the overall 'look' is ambiguous, even askew. Clothing, make-up, hairstyle etc is essentially a collage, each component taken up on the level of the fashion equivalent of the ready made – as *2nd hand*. [21]

Posers were their own art object, their own art theory (ten years earlier Bruce Maclean had formed Nite Style: the World's First Pose Band, 'not theatre, not dance, not mime, not rock or art, but pose, a context of its own'). [22] This was McLaren's theory of 'disruptive' fashion given a myriad individual versions; like Andrew Logan's Miss World parties, it was an art school dance, everyone obsessed with visual detail, every clothes choice an artistic gesture. A curl worn here, a belt as well as braces, stockings instead of tights, yellow shoes, trousers with turn-ups; everything had meaning. The implication of this New Romantic movement was that each individual consumer choice is a creative act, an argument followed through most brilliantly by the fashion fanzine *i-D*, put together by St Martin's students and ex-students, with its pages of photos of passersby, snapped and grilled about why they're wearing chains/ pinstripes/Oxfam/jeans/furs, until even the most 'normal' appearance becomes a matter of wonder. *i-D* was the still equivalent of the art school dance: *everyone* is posed.

For a moment art school theories of subversive consumption had a pop presence. We discuss the sociological reasons for this further in chapter 5 but it is important to stress here that the impact of art school music always depends on wider cultural circumstances. The 1960s rock bohemians found fame by riding the new waves of middle-class Anglo-American youth culture; the pop situationists became stars because of late-seventies shifts in markets and marketing techniques. As mainstream rock products went on being made according to the various successful formulas (progressive rock, stadium rock, AOR, etc.) and mainstream dance music came to be dominated by producer-centred disco, so there developed an obvious need for new teen-aimed pop personalities. And there were, too, now new ways of reaching them. MTV, the USA's cable music-

young American audience since radio formats froze in the early 1970s. For the moment, then, 'subversive' pop, with its three-minute packed and packaged narratives of desire, had a sales impact. It didn't take long, of course, for new pop formulas to emerge, and the biggest British stars in America (Duran Duran, Billy Idol, Tears for Fears, Eurythmics) were the most old-fashioned, the most *rocking*, but in Britain, at least, 1981–2 was a wonderful time for theoretical stars. Musicians like Marc Almond and Green reread Pop art and punk in terms of the fragility of imagery, reheard soul and disco as the lineaments of desire; Barthes and Derrida were quoted in the *NME*; New Romanticism meant a new pop slogan – everyone, as a consumer, was equal.

The problem of this position wasn't that it was co-opted but that it was incoherent. For a start, it was difficult to see how 'subversiveness' came in. For the pop situationist consumption had to be disrupted, the radical artist placed a slow-acting fuse in the commodity itself (packaging records in sandpaper); now consumption was being celebrated, it was the moment when consumers realized themselves, and this argument was indistinguishable from that of advertising – the joy of consumption defined in terms of the 'value' of the commodity (and vice versa). And so *The Face* became the hip consumer guide to the eighties, peddling pop situationism and pop structuralism as market styles like Levi's 501s, even its acerbic political commentary reading like a socialism that could change as fast as one's hair-do.

The 'equality' of consumption was never a happy slogan for art school students anyway. If creativity came into play only at the moment of market choice, then superior creativity must be indicated by superior market choices – students' claims to artistic status depended on their displays of style, their visual expertise was indicated by what they bought, how they dressed, where they shopped. The professional clothes-makers of Sex had mischievously sold an 'amateur' look, the art student's concern now was to be obviously professional.

In the early days of Blitz, as Rosetta Brooks suggested, clique approval was all that a good pose needed (on the streets the visible frissons of shock were, to begin with, compensation enough for the work of making oneself up), but this was not a situation that could last. Many of the Blitz crowd were, anyway, as fashion and design students, seeking recognition in career terms, from teachers and potential employers and customers, and even those who weren't could, in the end, only validate their 'creativity' through a *positive* public response. The New Romantics weren't a youth subculture like the skinheads or even punks, content to look 'odd' or menacing. They wanted acknowledgement of their *individual* style, and having defined their creativity through commodities, they could only be properly appreciated if they were themselves consumed. As Rimmer points out, the posers at the Blitz weren't just dressing up, they were dressing up and *pretending to be famous* – their 'individuality' only made sense when it had a public effect; they had, indeed, invented themselves at second hand, as if they were images projected by other people: 'Punk had applied the anyone-can-do-it idea to the process of forming a band and becoming famous; the new romantics ditched the trappings and applied it to fame, pure and simple. Forming a band came later.'[23]

Sixties beat musicians and seventies punks alike had wanted to make music in the first place not as a college project but because they heard in blues and rock and roll a unique means of expressing themselves and energizing their listeners. They may have started out with a particular creative self-confidence, but our interest in this book has been what happens to pop music (made as confidently by thousands of non-art students) subsequently, when it becomes the object of the 'art attitude'; we've never doubted art school musicians' commitment to their music in the first place. But for the Blitz poseurs music itself was always a secondary issue. Music-making was now only a means to an end; commercial and aesthetic success were measured by the same criteria. Image, as Adam Ant, the first star to make the move from punk to new pop, realized, was all that he had to sell; to be a pop star, as Boy George found out, meant to be a Pop Star, all performances – on stage, in bed, for the press, with Terry Wogan – performance art (and Boy George thus played his fall with the same *brio* he had played his rise). For the new pop acts it was not a question of making good music then marketing it; it was skill in the sales process that made the music 'good'. As a singer, for example, Sade was inconceivable except as a star. Artistic and commodity status had become the same thing, and even the avant-garde was now designed,

This is a RECORD COVER. This writing is the DESIGN upon the
record cover. The DESIGN is to help SELL the record. We hope
to draw your attention to it and encourage you to pick it up.
When you have done that maybe you'll be persuaded to listen to
the music - in this case XTC's Go 2 album. Then we want you
to BUY it. The idea being that the more of you that buy this
record the more money Virgin Records, the manager Ian Reid and
XTC themselves will make. To the aforementioned this is known
as PLEASURE. A good cover DESIGN is one that attracts more
buyers and gives more pleasure. This writing is trying to pull
you in much like an eye-catching picture. It is designed to get
you to READ IT. This is called luring the VICTIM, and you are
the VICTIM. But if you have a free mind you should STOP READING
NOW! because all we are attempting to do is to get you to read
on. Yet this is a DOUBLE BIND because if you indeed stop you'll
be doing what we tell you, and if you read on you'll be doing what
we've wanted all along. And the more you read on the more you're
falling for this simple device of telling you exactly how a good
commercial design works. They're TRICKS and this is the worst
TRICK of all since it's describing the TRICK whilst trying to
TRICK you, and if you've read this far then you're TRICKED but
you wouldn't have known this unless you'd read this far. At
least we're telling you directly instead of seducing you with
a beautiful or haunting visual that may never tell you. We're
letting you know that you ought to buy this record because in
essence it's a PRODUCT and PRODUCTS are to be consumed and you
are a consumer and this is a good PRODUCT. We could have
written the band's name in special lettering so that it stood
out and you'd see it before you'd read any of this writing and
possibly have bought it anyway. What we are really suggesting
is that you are FOOLISH to buy or not buy an album merely as a
consequence of the design on its cover. This is a con because
if you agree then you'll probably like this writing - which is
the cover design - and hence the album inside. But we've just
warned you against that. The con is a con. A good cover design
could be considered as one that gets you to buy the record, but
that never actually happens to YOU because YOU know it's just a
design for the cover. And this is the RECORD COVER.

'The triumph of design'

like Richard Strange's Cabaret Futura, to *signify* the avant-garde.
The charts, following the success of Kid Creole, became open to
pastiche and mixed-up versions of every pop style under the sun.

If Pop art was the revenge of graphics on fine art, New Pop was
the triumph of design. Post-punk musicians' concern to supervise
their own packaging (Jerry Dammers, for instance, seemed as proud
of his 2-Tone logo as of the Specials' music), was now translated into
the language of the 'corporate image'; subversive pop was turned
inside out. Manchester art students Peter Saville (Factory's original
designer) and Malcolm Garrett (who began his pop work with the
Buzzcocks) pioneered an approach in which 'each and every mani-

festation of an artist – a record sleeve, a T-shirt, a badge – would be clearly identifiable as part of an overall design scheme'. In his work for Duran Duran, Garrett produced 'record sleeves, books, shirts, badges, brochures and even a board game for the group, all stamped with the logo of his company, Assorted Images'. His company partner, Kasper de Graaf, suggested that 'the innovations in packaging and design and so forth over the last seven or eight years have been in pop music in Britain. There are lots of other really good artists around the world but for corporate identity and all that implies, Britain is where it's at.' Among these innovations, it turned out, was punk. By 1985 the punk 'look', as the agencies understood it, the graphics and typography appropriated by designers like Neville Brody at *The Face*, had become the hottest language in advertising:

> 'What these magazines have done is make us all more aware of the street; they have given the street credibility,' says John Hegarty, creative inspiration at Bartle, Bogle, Hegarty. 'Much of what is in these mags is unreadable but the message is not what you say but how you look; they have been revolutionary and we are trying to adapt what they have been doing . . . '[24]

Natural practices/unnatural acts

The thing that makes *Parallel Lines* assuredly avant-garde is precisely that it's so airtight and multiple-varnished, such a pristinely slick piece of product that it's not even vapid like Barry Manilow, who at least can embarrass/make you throw up once in a while with an 'At the Copa'. Nope. This is it. The masterpiece. Gotta be, because its dimensions are so perfect: no bottom, no top, no sides, no rides, no new nows no how. Each song is a perfectly constructed concave system in which every single piece of information offered up in the lyrics cancels out another corresponding piece of information, kinda like a jigsaw puzzle except at the end instead of a picture you get a perfect blank. And that blank of course is nothing less than Deborah Harry's face. (Lester Bangs)[25]

In mass cultural theory the separation of high and low culture really means different critical terms: high art is good or bad, low art authentic or inauthentic. Rock and roll has conventionally been

discussed in terms of its truth value, as a struggle between spontaneous expression and the falsifying moves of the music industry.
Read any rock history, from Charlie Gillett's account of the rise and
fall of 1950s rock 'n' roll, *The Sound of the City*, to Dave Rimmer's in-
sider account of the New Pop, *Like Punk Never Happened*, and you
find the same narrative line: the initial rush of popular energy; the
routinizing record company response. If postmodernism means a
breakdown of high/low cultural boundaries, it means too the end of
this historical myth – which is where the art–pop musicians come in,
complicating sociological readings of what music means, putting into play their own accounts of authenticity and artifice.

The original idea of rock authenticity came from a straightforward Romantic ideology of creativity. For the 1960s art school
beat musicians, true expression was defined against both bourgeois
and showbiz convention, and 'rock' was differentiated from 'pop'
along the axes of passion, commerce and complexity. But, from the
start, there was something more complicated going on here than the
simple artistic use of a new means of personal expression. The real
question was not whether these musicians could or should play the
blues (most British artists this century have used forms and techniques developed by other people in other circumstances) but how
anyone could tell if they did it well or not. Was the emotional force
of this music registered by the correct use of the original blues language (the purist line) or by its individuality – in which case at least
some gesture had to be made to the peculiarity of white boys and
girls singing black songs as a mark of their honesty.

The latter approach, which turned white blues into rock, meant
making music ironically – a singer like Mick Jagger seemed to stand
aside from his own performance – and acknowledging that blues
and rock are not British folk forms. British musicians made something new out of blues and rock and roll, a complex and expressive
form of pop, but, nevertheless, to play this way was to be *artful* (these
sounds didn't come to us naturally, were not ingrained in church or
pub or even radio) and so the problem they faced was that as their
music became popular, it was mediated through market relations
significantly different from those linking creator and consumer in
the art world. Rock was quickly recuperated by commerce, as the LP
replaced the single, the concert the package tour, the student

the teen audience, and, as Jon Stratton has shown, Romantic ideology thus became the ideology of the record industry itself:

> Romanticism, whilst lived as being in opposition to capitalist concerns founded on rationality and standardisation, in fact supports capitalism by providing both an enabling rationale for invention and a sustaining emphasis on the individual which allows cultural products to be viewed as something other than simply more commodities.[26]

But rock's co-option was not a simple matter either. By the early 1970s there may have been no contradiction between the rock roles of artist and entertainer, but there was something awry. The issue was how rock musicians should be *consumed*. Showbiz success had traditionally been defined in terms of the pleasure performers gave their fans, partly through the spectacle they made of themselves, partly through their force of personality. Stardom came from the tension between intimacy and distance, between performers' availability and their exoticism, and music was made to play on this – there was no significant difference between the stars themselves and their songs, between their 'real' and their 'stage' identity. Entertainers were, by their nature, transparent; honesty simply meant giving their audiences all they'd got.

This was the model too for Britain's first rock 'n' roll acts, for subsequent youth pop. Cliff Richard may have been a fake – Harry Webb dressed up as Elvis – but he was never artificial: his act was part of his personality. We're not expected to notice, let alone admire, Webb's performance as Richard as we were, say, Bryan Ferry's as 'Bryan Ferry' or even, as his act became more arty, John Lennon's as a Beatle. When the art school blues bands became pop stars they were then, glamorized, despite themselves, turned into personalities in the pages of *Rave* or *NME*. They did experience a gulf between what they 'really' were, artists, and what they were presented as being, pop boys. The progressive rockers responded by becoming as unglamorous as possible (which meant, in practice, developing new forms of 'serious' entertainment, a new genre of rock 'criticism'), but the Pop art pop stars became fascinated with their own 'image' (the term which replaced 'personality' in the language of marketing). Once more the 'authenticity' of pop art meant a concern for its

'. . . but he was never artificial'

(Photograph by Harry Hammond)

artificiality, and the audience was divided into the true fans, who could see through an act, and the mass consumers, who couldn't.

What we're describing here is the dialectic of authenticity and artifice that pop entails. In the 1960s the pursuit of authentic expression in the music market place meant an increasing interest in the inventions involved. In the 1970s it was, in turn, their concern with packaging and the sales process that most clearly registered musicians as 'true' artists – by the end of the 1970s, the more 'false' the image, the more obvious the cultural pretensions. The whole of the 1980s new pop movement, from Martin Fry's mocking account of his own personality as a matter of gestures to Trevor Horn's use of 'natural' noise and 'unnatural' hits in the mixes and remixes of Dollar, ABC, Malcolm McLaren and Frankie, rested on the display of conspicuous commercialism. If the avant-garde rock gesture in the late 1960s had been to make music to which no one could easily listen, the avant-garde pop gesture in the early 1980s was to make a product so tightly packaged that its meaning was exhausted in the act of purchase. Subversion was now a matter of form not content; even political interest moved from the forces of production to the moment of consumption. All that could be challenged now was 'meaning'.

There are a number of related reasons for this shift of interest – not just the punk flirtation with situationism and the art school influence of poststructuralist theory, but also a new recording and computer technology, the collapse of the idea of youth as a community, the discrediting of the progressive rock performer and audience as any sort of vanguard, the decline in live performance (see chapter 5) – but the replacement of a rock by a pop sensibility did not *solve* the problem of creativity in the market place. Rather, it altered the terms of commercial recuperation.[27]

Take something we've already mentioned, the development of *The Face*, the magazine founded in 1980 at the conjuncture of music, fashion, art and design. Its early juxtapositions of discourse were exciting; more clearly even than bands like ABC or Human League, *The Face* showed how pop style works – as a production, as a phantasm, as a source of skewed discontent and momentary carelessness. And then, slowly, the tone changed, grew more consistent, more self-congratulatory. By the time of the special fifth anniversary issue success was claimed as 'the credo of the decade' – *The Face*'s own

'So tightly packaged'

success (a circulation of 80,000 and rising), success as an intangible personal quality. The deconstruction of the sales process had become a breathy celebration of sales people. Art was a mythical term again, but applied now not to musicians but to designers and copy-writers.

The 1980s art pop story is full of ironies. The new pop stars, self-conscious frauds, tackily glamorous like Boy George, inspired a revival of old-fashioned pop gossip and 'true' stories. *The Face*, once a mocking style catalogue, became the house journal of the advertising industry. The rise of the video clip meant not some startling new dissolution of media boundaries but, rather, the incorporation of pop into the aesthetics of the soft sell. New pop was the art school version of postmodernism – in its cut-up of styles and media, its genre cross-references, its use of pastiche and parody, its dressing up of mass cultural forms with high cultural claims and vice versa, its combination of sensual and intellectual intrigue, its use of fragment-ation and distance as well as melody and beat. But these were surface pleasures and, in the end, the very smoothness of new pop consump-tion implied that all cultural goods and consumers are equal, that none of them could be subversive. Style offers only illusions of creativity – illusions, indeed, that in a capitalist world are a necessary part of the leisure process. Hidden are the material inequalities of lei-sure power, the unequal distributions of cultural capital, the ways in which the art school visual professionals have now got a vested interest in the market system.

And so the counter-arguments – the pursuit of *real* artistic auton-omy – come back into play. But before considering whether art is any longer possible, there is one more point to be made about the history of art school pop. Look carefully at the Blitz Kids and see their threads begin to unravel. The celebration of style has always meant distant views or excessive close-ups – live on the surfaces and the make-up is soon smudged. Put it another way: the problem for the Blitz Kids, as for the previous generations of art school poseurs, was sex. The art school dance might go on for ever but once the music starts the most careful look is dishevelled, the coolest gaze un-done by the awkward way the bodies move. It's for this reason that black music, from jazz to funk to hiphop, is on the art school dance curriculum in the first place – as the sound of 'natural' grace and 'raw' power, to carry the promise of sexual release.

Romantic bohemians have always equated individual and sexual 'freedom', emotional truth with 'letting it all hang out'. And they've always coded this in gender terms, with women as both the domestic threat and the empty body on which individual (male) desire is written. The 1960s underground, for example, used naked women as the symbols of 'play power' and they soon became standard trappings of rock visuals too. As Dominy Hamilton points out, by the mid-1970s, 'it had become very difficult to distinguish between nostalgia, glamour and soft pornography on album sleeves'.[28]

But this sort of men-together-outrageous-and-free bohemianism didn't really make sense of the art rock experience. Gail (Mrs Frank) Zappa comments that

> In the sixties the thing I think was the downfall of most groups is that they thought they were really doing something, really making a statement. And they were out there night after night playing to audiences of thirteen- and fourteen-year-old girls. How can you get any satisfaction out of that if you are a mature, responsible male?[29]

Mainstream stadium adolescent rock and roll soon ceased to be played by mature males anyway, but even this points up the paradox – this audience was increasingly made up of thirteen- and fourteen-year-old boys. What rock stars were up against was the sexualization of consumption – *they* were the objects of desire. Just as with other aspects of their 'personality', the only way to maintain some sense of control was to take charge of this process, to serve oneself up as fantasy, to become a dandy. And this was, in the end, to disrupt the behaviour assumptions of 'natural' sexuality – by the 1980s even 'raunchiness' was clearly a pose, and the most macho acts had become the most camp – heavy metal bands in sequins and mascara, David Lee Roth giggling at his own image, Freddie Mercury of Queen, a resplendent gay icon leading his hoards of bedenimed male youth, camp followers, in sentimental anthems of masculinity.

As the artificiality of the stars' own sexuality became apparent so too did the signs of gender. If in the 1960s naked women had stood for 'natural' sex, now clothed women, glamour girls, indicated the 'false' needs fed by mass production.[30] Roxy Music's Pop art works featured high fashion models like Jerry Hall and Amanda Lear, photographed to draw attention to the discomfort of their pose. The implication was no longer that if you were a star (if you were a man) you could have women like these (though if you were a *super* star you could!) but that as a star you *became* like this – a rich, haughty, unobtainable object of desire. These were 'sexy' images (*Country Life* had the women removed from its American sleeve) but presented without the sentimentality of bohemianism; not pin-ups but comments on pin-ups. And once pop stars began exploring the semiology of glamour, then women could employ their superior experience and expertise. Patti Smith's cover shot for *Horses* in 1975, for example (photo by Robert Mapplethorpe), 'cool and dispassionate as it is', manages, in Dominy Hamilton's words, 'to put across a message of ambiguous sexuality and arrogant decadence'. All this with the minimum of means – a man's casual shirt and tie, hands to breasts, homage to Keith Richards. [31]

Patti Smith, like David Bowie, had a significant influence on punk and she had a much more sophisticated understanding than him of gender codes. Because 'femininity' is made for the male gaze, so it is defined by a look, in the hang of one's clothes, the use of make-up, the angle of the camera. A man can dress up as a woman and create a thrill of unease from the obvious misconnection but the question will still be asked: what is his sexual taste *really*? His control of his situation is not in doubt; there is always someone behind what we see. Women can't dress up as men, only wear men's clothing; the *Horses* sleeve tells us nothing about Patti Smith, its messages concern her clothes, the imagery itself.

This was precisely the visual interest of punk, which from the start raised questions about sexual codes. It is often argued that punk opened a space which allowed women in – with its debunking of 'male' technique and expertise, its critique of rock naturalism, its anti-glamour. But the spaces were there because of women's involvement in the first place. Punk *bricolage*, for example, was most effective in the work of Vivienne Westwood and Poly Styrene, in the play of the female art school musicians on images of femininity. Iconography which is consistent in patriarchal ideology – woman as innocent/slut/mother/fool – was rendered ludicrous by *all being worn at once*.

If punk did give women (and art school women, in particular) new opportunities in pop it was not, then, as musicians as such (the 1980s return to electronic expertise meant the boys took back the toys) but as style experts – like Kim Wilde, Sade or Bananarama (two of whom graduated from the London College of Fashion). Male musicians like Marc Almond and Green might raise desultory questions about 'desire' but women performers have always had to think sharply about what their 'glamour' means, about sexuality as identity and commodity.

The most interesting commentary on this in pop terms was the late-seventies career of Deborah Harry's Blondie. Harry was in part a familiar sex object, the traditional American pin-up, a blonde fetish who presented herself in such a stylized way as to draw attention to the conventions that defined her. But, even more interestingly, she used this sort of Pop art performance to explore something else too – the relationship of the female consumer to this male-defined feminine ideal. Harry's glamour clothes were cheap glamour clothes, her gestures were awkward, her roots showed. And so she (and then Boy George and, most dramatically, Madonna) became a new sort of teenybop idol – someone for young girls to look like.

There are obvious parallels between Harry's project and New York artist Cindy Sherman's series of 'Film Stills' and 'Untitled' photographs. Both start from the premise that 'where femininity is concerned' the opposition between the 'real' and the 'artificial' has no meaning; both use their work to link 'the erotic and the vulnerable'. In her pictures Sherman plays The Woman in a series of pop narratives, a portrait of the artist-as-image. As Judith Williamson writes,

> 'Image' has a double sense, both as the kind of woman fantasized (is your 'image' aggressive, cute, femme fatale, dumb blonde, etc.), and as the actual representation, the photograph. What Sherman does is to make you see the type of 'woman', of femininity, as inseparable from the literal presentation of the image – lighting, contrast, composition, photographic style . . . The image suggests that there is a particular kind of femininity in the *woman* we see, whereas in fact the femininity is in the image itself, it *is* the image – 'a surface which suggests nothing but itself, and yet in so far as it suggests there is something behind it, prevents us from considering it as a surface'[32]

(Photograph by Chris Stein)

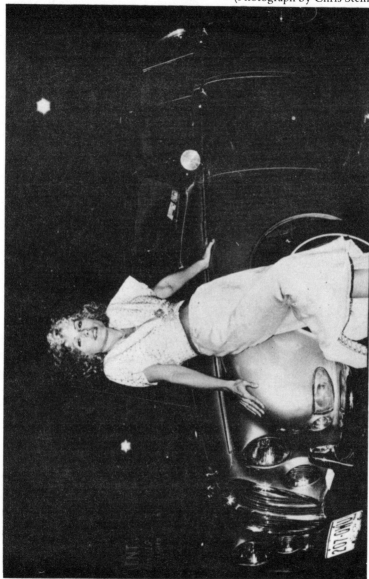

'The opposition between . . .'

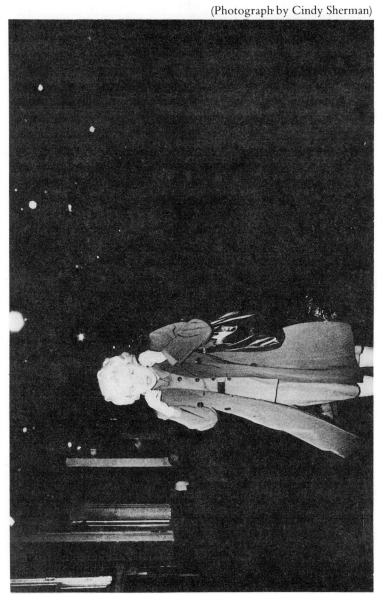

(Photograph by Cindy Sherman)

'... the real ....'

(Photograph by Chris Stein)

'. . . and the artificial . . . '

ZG

No 7

80p $3·00

DESIRE

(Photograph by Cindy Sherman)

'. . . has no meaning'

Art/Pop art/pop seem to meet up here and yet Cindy Sherman's pictures, whatever their pop sources, hang in galleries, feature in art magazines. They *are* considered as surfaces; they're art works. And Deborah Harry's image, whatever its sources, was, in the end a sales device, something to be used (and used up).

5
ART AND POP REVISITED

August 25, 1985: Green Gartside of Scritti Politti is interviewed in the *Sunday Times* magazine. Of all the art school punks he has made the most barefaced transition from Marxisant do-it-yourself disruption to professional self-manufacture. 'Before having his picture taken for this article,' writes Green's interviewer, Stephen Fay, 'a fee had to be negotiated with Virgin Records for his make-up artist.'[1]

Late May, 1986: Factory Records announce their latest product:

> Back in July 1976 Malcolm McLaren, Ray Rossi and Richard Boon promoted a concert at the Lesser Free Trade Hall in Manchester which was part of the explosion that became punk. To celebrate the 10th anniversary of that new music from the North West of England we now have '*FAC 151/THE FESTIVAL OF THE 10TH SUMMER*', a week of events to take place in Manchester.

The week was divided under ten headings: Art (an installation by Peter Saville Associates), Design (an exhibition co-ordinated by Assorted Images), Film and Video, Photography, Music, Fashion and Merchandizing (the poster, the T-shirt, the badge, the overall.)[2]

For Factory Records too the situation had changed. The ten years since punk had made the pop concert, the art event, the fashion show, the video clip and the sales pitch all the same thing. By September 1986 Frank Owen was reporting in an *i-D* education special that 'Jocelyn Stevens has recently given the go-ahead to a Department of Pop Music to be housed at the RCA under the guidance of Laurence Gane, a Senior Lecturer in the Department of Cultural History'. As Owen made clear, this was a hard-nosed decision (Stevens 'wouldn't have given the say-so to something that was an obvious economic flop'). These days it is as obvious to art college administrators as to their students that music-making offers an answer to the question of the 1980s art school career.[3]

The Romantic commodity

This question is more pressing than ever because of the Thatcher government's attempt to reduce public spending on higher education and to bring market forces into play in the subsequent distribution of scarce resources. For art education (as we discussed in chapter 2) this has had two specific consequences. First, 'restructuring' – as planned by the newly constituted National Advisory Body for Public Sector Higher Education – means consolidation, rationalization, a specialist division of teaching labour within the Polytechnic sector. Farewell to the independent art school. Second, the market orientation means favouring Design over Fine Art courses (cut by 20 per cent) and, within design education itself, a new emphasis on 'flexibility'. The NAB, like the MSC in its organization of other school-leaver training, is keen on the idea of 'transferable skills'.

In art schools 'the cuts' have meant a bitter rerun of old debates about the proper relationship of pure and applied training. For teacher-painters, sculptors and performance artists the 'use' of their departments is self-evident: they are the laboratories in which design ideas and attitudes are first developed. For the applied arts staff (and 90 per cent of art school courses are now design-centred) traditional fine arts departments are, equally clearly, conservative, staffed by people (mostly male, white people) for whom teaching is a secondary activity. The myth of creativity has been a convenient excuse for their failure to promote the public appreciation of art, artists or art schools.[4]

163

From this perspective fine artists have only themselves to blame for their bad image – boozy, bohemian, elitist, and thus vulnerable to commercial operators like Jocelyn Stevens. Frank Owen, going further, suggests that Romantic ideology itself, the bid for freedom from social forces, has been 'useless as a defence against Thatcherite austerity'. But this is to forget that Romanticism has always been a necessary component of the bourgeois world view too, a crucial aspect of commodity aesthetics. As we argued in chapter 2, applied artists – designers – are 'relevant' to industry precisely because of their ability to apply Romantic tenets to everyday market relations. The peculiarity of capitalism is that its reason for being – the buying and selling of goods – rests on exchanges which are equal (each side must want what the other offers: money, a commodity) but unequal (what is being sold is not what is being bought). Buyers want to satisfy needs, to achieve particular use-values; sellers are concerned simply to convert their commodities into cash, to realize their exchange-value. Marx's original point was that as capitalism develops, use-value is subordinated to exchange-value; production decisions are determined by profit possibilities, not by what societies and people actually need. But exchanges must still take place, consumers must still think that their purchases are useful, and so, in W.F. Haug's words, what capitalists now produce is a seeming use-value: 'the aesthetics of the commodity in its widest meaning – the sensual appearance and the conception of its use-value – becomes detached from the object itself.'[5]

From this conventional Marxist perspective, the commodity promises use-value, courts and fascinates us, but, once bought, turns out to be an illusion. Goods may have a use – Hoovers pick up dust – but not the use we bought them for: effortless housework, a *change* in our lives. The moment when we feel most clearly ourselves – when we make our market choices – turns out to be the moment when we are most at the mercy of society. In Judith Williamson's words, 'passions born out of imbalance, insecurity, the longing for something *more*, find forms in the objects and relations available; so that energies fired by what might be, become the fuel for what is.' This is, in Marxist terms, commodity fetishism. Our individuality is guaranteed by our taste; our creativity by our consumption, and, in Laura Kipnis's words, this means that the discourse of advertising is itself constituted by the rhetoric of imagination, rebellion, creativity and free expression that was once associated primarily with the figure of the artist. To become the quintessential artistic subject you do not have to paint your masterpiece, but only consume the right stuff. This once oppositional language, originating in the Romantic invention of the artistic subject, has achieved a dubious universality. In postmodernism, the artistic subject produced in high art, in mass culture, in advertising *and* consumption *is* the bourgeois subject.[6]

For art school students the universality of Romantic ideology has had two immediate consequences. First, creative authority is increasingly expressed through original consumption, a superior *pose* (this comes out again and again in the capsule student interviews in *i-D* – their art works are rarely mentioned). Second, art students have become experts in the *idea* of creativity (the 'conception of use-value' in Haug's terms), and the fine/applied art opposition is therefore misleading. If nothing else, the 1955-65 reform of British art education meant developing a 'fine art attitude' (the Coldstream phrase) in *all* students – this was the time when 'Basic Design' became a means for free expression.[7]

This has significant implications for current accounts of postmodernism. As Scott Lash and John Urry point out, postmodern culture is taken to describe a situation in which art has lost its aura (modernism was the final 'auratic' movement). Postmodern art cannot be set apart from market values or made accessible only to the properly educated. It isn't interpreted but experienced; it plays on the senses of the distracted passer-by. Iain Chambers, following up Walter Benjamin's suggestion that mechanical reproduction has 'liberated creativity *from* art', thus celebrates postmodern culture as

the disruptive ingression of popular culture, its aesthetics and intimate possibilities, into a previously privileged domain. Theory and academic discourses are confronted by the wider, unsystematized, popular networks of cultural production and knowledge. The intellectual's privilege to explain and distribute knowledge is threatened . . . The world has moved on. It is no longer necessarily tied to traditional discourses, institutions and voices for information about its meaning.[8]

We have great sympathy with Chambers' position, which echoes the arguments of 1950s Pop art theorists like Richard Hamilton that the aesthetic decisions made in the act of consumption are every bit as interesting as those made by fine artists in their secluded studios. The problem that tends to be elided by Chambers, though, is that popular culture is market culture, 'popular networks of cultural production and knowledge', are popular networks of consumption. This is why more orthodox socalist theorists take a much gloomier view of affairs. For Todd Gitlin, for example, what postmodernism means is that 'blank expression and flat appearance come together in a common chord which resounds through contemporary culture like a great dead sound.' For Gitlin, as for Fredric Jameson, postmodern pastiche and parody and *bricolage* reflect not a democratic challenge to traditional authority but the denial of *any* authority except that of multinational capital. When there is no such thing as the coherent self, the authentic voice, then politics, as well as art, is impossible. [9]

The problem of such gloomy arguments is that they reveal (and disguise) the writers' own position as spectators, their own response to displacement, their own loss of cultural authority. It's as if academics remain in their ivory tower but surrounded now by images not books, their window on the world a TV screen, their experience a simulation of everyone else's, and Chambers is right to argue that for the rest of us consumption is a more complicated, more exhilarating affair, a source of both anxiety and excitement.

The terms of this debate are most obvious in the growing literature on pop videos, the most accessible form of postmodern art, available at home twenty-four hours a day. 'Why MTV?' asks the editor of a special MTV issue of the *Journal of Communication Inquiry*. Because 'we wish to locate, and perhaps dislocate, the debate between modernism and postmodernism in the world (on the screen) of everyday life.' 'MTV is orgasm,' explains John Fiske,

> When signifiers explode in pleasure in the body in an excess of the physical. No ideology, no social control can organise an orgasm. Only freedom can. All orgasms are democratic: all ideology is autocratic. This is the politics of pleasure. The signifiers work through the senses on the body to produce pleasure and freedom; the signifieds produce sense in the mind for ideology and control.

The rock video is, it seems, television's 'only original art form'. [10]

What's bizarre about such statements (and Fiske, at least, is claiming MTV for some residual anti-bourgeois revolution) is how much they read like the video-makers' own propaganda. Fiske finds 'freedom' in precisely those elements of rock videos which situate them as commercials (and his argument is just as applicable to ads for cars, Levis, etc.). As Julien Temple explains, more mundanely:

> What 'Bohemian Rhapsody' did do was coincide with the end of the record selling boom of the Sixties and early Seventies. What marks the development of the pop promo from then on is its increasing importance to an industry desperate to continue selling records. Many of the dinosaur rock stars of the early Seventies have used video as a life support system, prolonging their careers beyond their natural deaths, by pumping thousands of dollars into their promosexual mini-epics. [11]

Music videos are far from being free-floating signifiers. They are rooted in cinematic, televisual and commercial codes of desire, just as all performed music has its associated visual significance – how else did Elvis Presley become a star? As Jody Berland comments, it is only in rare cases that the potential disjunction between sound and image is actually realized by music videos. For the most part they're designed to reassert the authenticity, the rootedness of performance – 'the rock performer plays himself, and promises a continuity of self with the space beyond the stage. Among the successful, it takes a rare musician not to look like a video quotation of the image of a musician.' In their use of familiar codes videos thus give intellectual as well as sensual pleasure. 'People still need to feel that they "possess" the meaning of what is directed to them; part of the pleasure of reception is the feeling of competence, a recognition of the code that is, must be, made for them.' Music videos work, in short, as 'a form of semantic flattery'.

And some images are particularly potent. The image of the young-male-musician-with-guitar can mean, in a single flash, everything: bobby sox, punching out the boss, hitting the road, opposing the war, an old Chevy, 1958 in Kansas, dancing till dawn, coming on – this condensation of symbols (multileveled and elusive, like the music but clear, adamant) performing the performance of a performer which can speak each or any of these without speaking at all. [12]

The video-makers' skill rests on the economy (not the anarchy) of signs, on the use of visual stereotypes, narrative clichés and generic pop codes to set a place for the spectator. Video-makers are Pop artists – taking plunder from high art and mass culture alike – with a purpose: to position viewers as consumers. The most self-consciously postmodern video is thus designed to flatter the most self-consciously postmodern record buyer – 'I think we've made the sort of film we could have found on a skip', boasted the producer of the brilliant clip for Art of Noise's 'Close to the Edit'. That was, after all, ZTT's brief. [13]

The point we're making here is that what makes pop videos postmodern is not their 'exploding signifiers' but their equation of art and commerce: their aesthetic effect can't be separated from their market effect; the desires they address can't be realized except in exchange. Pop videos situate the viewer as both immediate spectator and would-be consumer, offering a social pleasure that depends on both direct visceral response and shared ideological identity – just as late-nineteenth-century department stores organized desires socially in their floor and window displays. The best videos, as Pat Aufderheide suggests, like any other good advertisements, arouse longings that can't be met, only fed by endless purchase – even McDonald's 'has installed monitors at many cash registers, offering tempting *images* of food'. The recurring message from MTV is that personal identity is a matter of fashion and, indeed, the fashion industry has been quick to realize the point of pop video:

Since 1977, when Pierre Cardin began making video recordings of his fashion shows, designers have been incorporating video into their presentations. Videos now run continuously in retail store windows and on floor displays. For many designers, what sells records already sells fashion, and some foresee a fashion channel. The Cooperative Video Network, a television news service, already offers a half-hour program, *Video Fashion News*, with three-minute segments on current designer models. Some designers regard video as a primary mode of expression. Norma Kamali

now shows her work only on video, both in stores and on pro-
grams. One of her best-known works is a video called 'The
Shoulder Pad Song'. [14]

The 'death of the author' in high culture means the cult of the
author in mass culture, as we all wear signed goods as a mark of
exclusivity and stars are made out of the blank bodies that appear in
advertisements. Just as the success of the mass market – everyone is
the same – depends on each person's individual impulse to be different, so the triumph of consumption depends on the continuing
Romantic belief in creative market power and the individual voice.
In the end the postmodern debate concerns the *source* of meaning –
not just its relationship to pleasure (and, in turn, to the source of that
pleasure) – but its relationship to power and authority. Who now
determines significance? Who has the right to interpret? For pessimists and rationalists like Jameson the answer is multinational capital – records, clothes, films, TV shows, etc. are simply the results of
decisions about markets and marketing. For pessimists and irration-
alists, like Baudrillard, the answer is nobody at all – the signs that
surround us are arbitrary. For optimists like Iain Chambers and
Larry Grossberg the answer is consumers themselves, stylists and
subculturalists, who take the goods on offer and make their own
marks with them. [15]

What interests us, though, is that these 1980s writers (unlike
1950s Pop theorists) discount the artists and musicians who actually
design cultural commodities as the source of their value. This is particularly striking in discussions of popular music, which is validated,
if at all, in terms of subcultural theory, even though few youth subcultures express themselves this way. Our point is that it is misleading to celebrate rock as amateur art, not just because all successful
rock (and punk and reggae and hiphop) musicians are in fact professionals, but also because pop meaning is the result of a different sort
of art/commerce dialogue. The issue is not the co-option of a street
sound or style by commerce (and commercial musicians) or the
liberation of a commercial sound or style by 'the kids', but how
'truth' and 'subjectivity' and 'uniqueness' are registered in normal
market relations themselves. And to grasp what's going on here we
have to pay proper attention to the music-makers.

The artist as producer

The importance of art school pop stars is not their disdain for the profession of music but their engagement with the profession of art. This is the context in which the postmodern evaporation of aura has become a *practical* issue. In what is perhaps the most dramatic denial of creative authority, for example, the American artist Sherry Levine simply steals other people's 'original' photographic images and presents them as her own. Her photographs of photographs offer exactly the same visual pleasures as the originals but 'in deconstructing the sister notions of origin and originality' act to 'void the basic propositions of modernism, to liquidate them by exposing their fictitious condition'. The paradox, as Thomas Lawson points out, is that the myth of personal vision (and Levine steals the most conventionally 'arty' imagery of such photographers as Eliot Porter and Edward Weston) has its own sneaky resilience: 'The extremity of her position doubles back on her, infecting her work with an almost romantic poignancy as resistant to interpretation as the frank romanticism of her nemesis.'[16] For Levine (as for the more stylized photographic 'thief', Cindy Sherman) the impossibility of personal art has become the source of a new Romantic statement – Levine and Sherman's work is still signed, shown, bought and sold. An alternative, less poignant response to the postmodern situation, the Warhol way, is to turn artist into star, to replace Romantic aura with bright commercial vibes. Robert Hughes suggests that Warhol's artistic credibility in the 1960s came from his 'ghostly aura of power' over his Superstars. Their function was to be Warhol's fans, projecting onto him their own desires, dressing up to be reflected in his shades. Valerie Solanas, notes Hughes, shot Warhol because 'he had too much control over her life'. The obsessive Barry Manilow, Bowie and Nick Heyward fans interviewed by Fred and Judy Vermorel in *Starlust* felt themselves similarly possessed.[17]

For a later generation of New York artists, more single-minded than Warhol, more confident and, most importantly, more familiar with the ways of rock stardom ('all the people who wanted to be musicians in the late seventies now seem to be whittling their drumsticks into paint brushes'), selling oneself as a brand image is more straightforward. Keith Haring, for example, on advice from Warhol, has opened

a store, in which he sells posters, shirts, buttons and basically himself. Some say this is an outrageous sell-out – artists shouldn't
mass-market their work in boutiques. Haring insists it's a gene-
rous act that makes his work accessible to the public at reasonable
prices. It also helps him control his own merchandise and fight
those counterfeiters who've turned up everywhere from Australia
to Greece. [18]

Both Sherry Levine and Keith Haring reject the belief that an image
can be 'immediately readable and meaningful in and of itself, regardless of its context or of the circumstances of its production, circulation,
and reception'. The point we'd stress is that while much postmodern
argument has derived from linguistic theory and literary criticism –
from studies of languages in which elements of meaning are 'relatively arbitrary in regard to their referents in the real world' – postmodern fine art practice has to take account of 'iconicity', the
resemblance of units of visual meaning to the real world. Images are
seen and the analysis of art (like the analysis of film, television and
performed music) has to take account of 'distinct communicative
situations, particularly conditions of reception, enunciation, and
address, and thus, crucially, the notion of *spectatorship*'. [19]

It is precisely this concern for spectatorship, the social relations of
consumption, that art school graduates bring into pop practice –
they are, to adapt Peter Fuller's words, 'metavisual professionals' –
and share with their fellow graduates in advertising agencies,
fashion houses and video studios. Their problem, to put it another
way, is not whether or not to 'sell out' (to switch from artistic to
commercial logic) but how to set up a relationship with an audience,
a market, that is somehow different from a straight sales pitch, that
confirms their status as 'artists'.

If fine art is the 'laboratory' for design techniques, how can fine
artists avoid being implicated in a business process from the moment
they first put brush to canvas? It is, indeed, easy enough to interpret
rock, in particular, as the model for the general development of post-
war consumer society. It first constructed the key ideological markets – 'youth', 'the counter-culture', 'subcultures', 'stylists'; it first
came up with the value of being 'with-it', first defined community as
'taste-public', lives as 'life-styles'. At each stage art school musicians

had an important role to play. In their very sense of themselves as rock artists, as a pop avant-garde, they designed the ideal record *consumer* (as Hamilton had suggested), the person who had to keep visiting the shops, attending the concerts, reading the *NME*, just to stay different. [20]

The work of music in the age of electronic production

Ideologically art school musicians are artists, practically they are musicians – music is what they *do* – and music-making poses its own problems of authority and audience. For a start, in the music world the boundaries between 'high' and 'low' forms are still carefully patrolled. The (relatively few) musicians regularly cited as bridging pop and the musical avant-garde turn out to have their own art school connections (whether British studio experimentalists like Brian Eno and David Cunningham, American performance artists like Laurie Anderson, or German electronic groups like DAF) while the musical avant-garde itself – exemplified by Pierre Boulez – has no interest in pop ideas at all. [21]

Postmodern issues have a different historical trajectory in music than in the visual arts. If composers and painters faced similar problems of audience, market and social purpose at the turn of the century (which meant a common 'modernist' movement) the effects of mechanical reproduction have been different – musicians have not been faced with quite the same questions of realism and representation. Indeed, it can be argued that for 'popular' musicians it was recording technology itself that gave them artistic status (hence the 'aura' of blues, jazz and rock) while even 'classical' musicians were not threatened by records in the same way artists were threatened by photographs. It is only in the last decade, with the development of electronic and computer-programmed instruments and recording devices, that the musician's authority, as composer and performer, has come into doubt (and the threat to 'live' sound and the 'finished' product is a problem too for record companies' use of Romantic ideology to justify musical property and the copyright system). [22]

Current angst in the music world seems, then, in fine art terms, oddly old-fashioned. Technology is seen to threaten not creative status but creative practice or what Peter Fuller once called the 'joy of labour'. 'I think we may have to accept that William Morris was right; machines may be useful to us for all sorts of things. They are, however, fundamentally incompatible with true aesthetic production.'[23] What machines destroy, in Fuller's terms, is the experience of working on 'raw' material and this point is taken up by Chris Cutler in his case against the latest technological devices for music-making, those 'electronic instruments designed and programmed to deliver readymade musical "units" at the press of a switch or touch on a pad, making "professional", fully formed "perfect" sounds or sequences available instantly.'[24] These machines 'deskill' musicians, turn musical producers into musical consumers:

> Of course we are not there yet and we may never be, quite, but the general principle and the mechanisms are all in place and exert a measurable influence on successive generations of music-makers. The older, out-dated model: of learning to play and slowly working your way up, finally to emerge, skilled, into reward and recognition (paying your dues as it used to be called) has long since been forgotten and abandoned for today's more comfortable model (ubiquitous in all spheres of fast-turnover fashion) of springing *straight from desire to 'expertise'* – as from obscurity to stardom, a phenomenon previously reserved for the unreal world of 'them' and Tin Pan Alley. Today's scenario is more democratic, and more magical. Its presiding deities are Luck (yours) and Cash (hopefully somebody else's), overshadowing yesterday's faith-objects: Application and Merit.[25]

Cutler's 'negative case' is interesting because it goes against the grain of most postmodern pop theory. He suggests that to open up music-making to all is, in practice, to limit what music can be made. The new units of composition are the 'standard' programmes of mass-produced computer instruments, the sounds 'found' in commercial practice. Learning music ceases to be a social activity, a matter of experiment with one's instrument and fellow musicians, and becomes 'an essentially solitary discipline, whose concerns are primarily "objective" and quantitative'. Hence the new sort of alienated 'art' musician.

Brian Eno's 'positive case' for the new technology fills out this picture. 'What's happened in music in the last thirty years', he suggests, 'is that new instruments have been continuously invented'.

There are now electronic machines that make the sounds of new musical instruments. You can just say, for example, 'I want an instrument that has sharp attack and a long decay of the sound, with the upper harmonics increasing as the decay goes on.' With a little programming you can have it. And then there are the recording studios, where you can take finite sounds and treat them as if their parameters were infinite. You can change the pitch to any extent you want, and you can change the timbre completely, change the duration, make it endlessly long or very short. Most of what pop music has been doing is experimenting with all this. . . . The interest today isn't in developing serial music or polyphony or anything like that. It is in constantly dealing with new textures.

Consumer devices like the Sony Walkman are also changing our use of sound: 'We call it music because it comes in through the ears, but it is very different from, say, Beethoven. It's made differently, played differently, heard differently.' Musicians now have to think in terms of soundscapes. Listeners are increasingly using music to create their own moveable locations, while record producers use the studio to construct sound 'as happening in a particular type of space'. Either way, making and listening to music are becoming more lonely activities, something which, as an artist, Eno anyway takes for granted: 'I'd like people to have the expectations of music that they presently have of painting.'[26]

The problem of computer music (a problem for Boulez in his electronic lab, IRCAM, as well as for Cutler and Eno), is what it means to make something – to make it well – when the musical 'object' is no longer easy to define, and when the conventional distinctions between 'live' and recorded sound, between musicians and engineers, between composition and performance, between natural and unnatural noise, have all broken down. But if the musicians' debate thus raises old fine art questions about the *material* of production, it also makes clear that in practice threats to creative authority can only be met collectively, and if the art world – the nexus of galleries, critics, collectors, colleges, and glossy magazines – seems stronger than ever despite (or because of?) the difficulty of art, the post-electronic music world seems decidedly precarious. This partly reflects the greater importance collective work has for music-making than for art. Musican skills (like sports skills) have always been assessed in the act of collaboration; 'good' musicians can only be judged as such in their effects on each other (this is most obvious in an improvised form like jazz, but even academic composers depend on performers to realize their work). One of the most important ways, then, in which rock and pop musicians have sustained a belief in themselves as creators has been through the support of a peer group or cult audience which can be seen as making a properly 'artistic' (or non-commercial) assessment of their work. This has been particularly important for art school musicians, more aware than most people of the tensions involved. It's interesting to note, for example, that David Byrne, the most obviously postmodern of current US rock musicians, asked whether he makes 'art' or 'product' (his latest work being a record/ film/video/photo-text), replied 'I feel I'm successful when I combine both together, when people forget the distinction between the two. If I can do a video which can be artistically successful and still get shown on TV, then I've got the best of both worlds.'[27]

Authentically postmodern

What is interesting about Byrne's position is its underlying ambivalence – he wants to dissolve the distinctions between art and product, but he's conscious of working in two worlds and also wants his work to sustain a status independent of its sales success. What this implies (an implication even clearer in Chris Cutler's argument) is that there is indeed an art-music niche, that the market decisions of mass consumers can be set aside from the aesthetic judgements of peers. Read this way, Cutler's negative account of technology (echoed by many old 'progressive' rockers) is less a defence of creative autonomy than the pained protest of a threatened community.

The optimistic reading of postmodern culture suggests, as we've seen, that the collapse of traditional artistic authority and skill is what allows the displaced, fractured experience of the dispossessed to be, for the first time, symbolized. For Angela McRobbie, for example, postmodern culture is the culture of 'the new generation of intellectuals (often black, female or working class)', the culture of irregular employment, disrupted education and economic insecurity.[28] And from this perspective postmodernism is a threat to all art and music worlds, not just to the high art establishment but also to the bohemian alliance of fine art teachers, 'free' musicians, pub poets and avant-garde performance groups which since the mid-1960s has run its own honours system. Jeff Nuttall's comment on the effects of punk, a 1960s luminary passing judgement on the 1980s, is, indeed, illuminating:

> The popular music, relieved by tiny islands of surviving brilliance like Bowie and Dury, skids into shithouse-wall obscenity, nursery school harmonies and Boys' Brigade rhythms. Sexual freedom twists weirdly into a near dictatorship of homosexuals, despising the womb and the testicles, preaching alienation, isolation and masturbation, all of which are ritualised in the death of the dance.[29]

For 1960s nostalgics, post-punk/postmodern culture clearly represents the triumphs of artifice over art: 'For this is the Age of Parody, of bogusness,' Philip Norman begins an apocalyptic piece in, of all places, Murdoch's *Sunday Times*. 'Illusion holds us in the barely fretful grip of sleep under hypnosis.'[30] For 1980s optimists, by contrast, postmodern culture is actually speaking the 'truth' of capitalist experience for the first time. What's really going on, in other words, is the eruption of new springs of symbolic authority. The 'others' of high culture are also the 'others' of bohemian culture (women, non-whites, 'minorities'), those social groups who can claim access to true (because hitherto unpackaged) critical experience (often taken to be rooted materially in the body). Postmodern art is fragmented because postmodern life is; postmodern artists skim the surfaces of the metropolitan landscape because these are the surfaces on which we have to live. Artifice isn't the issue here – it's difficult, for example, to think of a more realistic, more *authentic*, work of art than Mary Kelly's *Post-Partum Document* – but, rather, the old Romantic search in a new commercial setting for expressive directness, feelings untrammeled. Even after the obvious postmodern pastiche of a Prince or Run DMC the hippest art school magazines thus still take black American music to be the sound of the streets. For a while Channel 4 pointed up the argument by running *The Chart Show*, wall-to-wall white pop videos, fragmented gestures, right after *Solid Soul*, wall-to-wall black dancers, real sweat.

What's most striking about contemporary culture, then, is not the impossibility of Romantic art but people's continuing belief in it, their determination to express themselves anyway. The pop music movement as we write, for example, more mood than mode, is the cult surrounding the peculiarly British 'shambling' bands. The shamblers, indie-stylists of cast-offs and tat, seem to signify a conscious deconstruction of all fashion imperatives, but their imagery is more sham than shambolic; like everything else in postmodern culture, it is carefully contrived. Simon Reynolds reveals the stylistic incentives of the 'Ladybirds and Start-Rite Kids':

> What's interesting is the way the indie scene doesn't revive, but *weaves* elements from different eras to create fresh meanings. This is because the future is No Future, the death of the *idea* of the future; there'll be no more Next Big Things, just an ever-after of pick 'n' mix plundering from the past. No more major waves in fashion, no uniforms to be conformed to exactly – instead, on each of us descends the freedom (or burden?) of being the author of our own identity, making stylistic choices to express not so much our inner selves as our allegiances and our fantasies about who we'd *rather* be. [31]

Indie-stylists are the spiritual successors to the student fans who consumed progressive rock in the early and mid-1970s. Shamblers, too, are students – from sixth forms, colleges, polys but, significantly, not usually from art schools. In their account of authenticity the indie charts are the only indicators of pop quality because they contain the only truly expressive music, the only groups *resistant* to fashion, commercialism and art school 'irony'. Nobody in the shambling scene smiles at the actual irony of The Mission – the quintessential 1968 band in 1986 – topping the indie charts with a Neil Young song.

From the shamblers' perspective it is the fragmentation of social categories, the very superficiality of postmodern culture, that enables us to find contemporary relevance in wholesale borrowing from previous styles and non-styles. The idea of clothes as sexual display can be reworked to present an image of flatness itself – even the joins and contours of the body disappear. Reynolds again:

The crucial thing to note about this current indie-style (a mixture of pre-permissive, virtually pre-youth culture clothes and children's garments) is that it doesn't accentuate the shape of the figure: it conceals the signs of sexual difference and of adulthood. Just as indie-pop defines itself against chart pop, so indie-style defines itself against High Street fashion: music and style are a revolt against the sophistication and hyper-sexuality of mainstream pop culture, a revolt into innocence.[32]

Reality and its discontents

There is one more strand in this story we want to pull out, one more issue that has confused recent pop theory. In their own way (the revolt into innocence) these shambling bands reflect the breakdown of the taken-for-granted relationship between pop music and youth culture, the origins of which lie in the late 1970s, when the record industry faced a crisis (a stagnation in record sales after twenty years of expansion) brought on by the coincidence of two developments: on the one hand, an economic recession which hit particularly hard a most important sector of the record-buying market, working-class youth; on the other hand, technological developments in the leisure industry which meant new sorts of competition for people's leisure resources (home computers and video recorders were becoming as significant in people's lives as record players) and disrupted record companies' profit-making routines. (Home taping became the industry's chief bogey.)

The record industry's response to this situation was not particularly systematic but by now the trends are obvious: the average age of the pop market (and especially the pop single-buying market) is younger than it was; record companies devote more attention to building big mainstream stars than to servicing a variety of musical tastes; stars are now conceived and sold as multinational, multimedia performers; there's been a steady decline in the significance of live music-making except as a promotional device. This is the world in which art students, particularly applied art students, turn out to be the youth group with the most 'relevant' skills, and come to exemplify the advertisers' imagery of youth-as-permanent-leisure (rather than youth-as-enforced-idleness). It's for this reason that in the

1980s it has become harder for art school musicians to define themselves as the grit rather than the oil in the production line. As
Malcolm Garrett puts it,

> In 1976, students refused to join advertising agencies, because
> they thought their work would get swallowed and not be seen.
> Now advertising agencies rush down to college shows every year
> to snap up the best students. Thanks to punk, clients are realising
> you have to keep pace with youth style in order for products to
> sell. [33]

And the other side of the agencies' pursuit of students is students'
pursuit of agencies.

For sixties graduates like Jamie Reid the result is disturbing:

> Art schools are very different now. I can only judge it from per-
> sonal experience: last year I ended up by doing some teaching at
> Liverpool Art School and I was quite flabbergasted by the exper-
> ience. When I was at Art College I really didn't give a fuck; remem-
> ber it was the sixties and there was money around in Britain, so
> you were sheltered and privileged. You didn't care what you did
> at the end of it, so people took a lot more risks and there was, sup-
> posedly, more freedom. What amazed me last year – and it's to do
> with eight years of Thatcherism, it's to do with the cuts in educa-
> tion – is that the students are so frightened. They want to get the
> best passes they can, they want to get a job at the end of it – and to
> that extent they play safe and they play the game. I don't blame
> them, but it's a sad reduction in potential. [34]

There's nothing here to surprise mass culture critics – co-option
has always been the name of the commodity game, and the socialist
search for the incorruptible artist or artefact has always been doomed –
what, in the end, was 'subversive' about Pink Floyd or punk, Sade or
skiffle? For a while the impossibility of high art subversion – the end
of the avant-garde – meant socialists looking to the streets for whatever pockets of cultural resistance to capitalism remain, but if postmodern culture describes anything it describes a situation in which
the streets have no more 'autonomy' than the art galleries – the skin-
head hairstyle is no more or less 'fashionable' than David Bowie's.

What this suggests to us is not that we are all now colonized by advertisers' fantasies, but that the interplay of artifice and authenticity is central to *everyone's* lives in consumer capitalism. In looking at the shifting ways in which the love-hate relationship of the artist and society has been worked out in pop, we simply find the dialectic in graphic outline. The art pop story, in short, is not just a chronicle of defeats, but reveals how the terms of resistance and recuperation keep changing. Sixties art musicians' critique of pop commerce – the counter-culture – was thus recuperated through the rock star system, the musicians' creative authority sold to their fans as their own. Seventies art musicians' critique of the resulting rock commerce – pop situationism – was recuperated through the celebration of their commodity status itself. In both cases the Romantic urge to be different fuelled market mechanisms which ensured that everyone stayed the same, but in both cases the urge remained all powerful – for music-makers and consumers alike.

In telling this story we've been conscious of the pressure on us to take a line, to drop our academic pose. But if postmodern culture undermines cultural 'experts' (our judgements would be, anyway, arbitrary) it also means a new mode of consumption, a detached willingness to be impressed, and our faces are pushed up against the display windows just like everyone else's. The art/music story from this vantage is like one of those old-fashioned double-jointed, three-dimensional postcards. Look at it one way and see the story of surrender, the Romantic critiques of pop and rock dissolved in business deals. Shift position slightly and another picture can be glimpsed: the Romantic critique of pop becoming part of the pop process itself. In the end, then, we want to honour art school musicians for thirty years of music which has been funny, fascinating and, above all, argumentative. If art categories have been dissolved by commerce, commercial categories have been dissolved by art – Pop art pop stars, for example, mocked assumptions about sex and gender in both the charts *and* the galleries. For art school musicians (and critics and fans) themselves the problem now is to maintain their sense of superiority: when all aesthetic judgements are arbitrary only market decisions stick (and so *The Face* celebrates commercial success in its features pages while searching ever more feverishly for obscurity in its record reviews). But for the rest of us what has mattered and will matter most is the art school pursuit of *difference*.

Pop culture describes the peculiar way in which our most intense experience of ourselves as ourselves (active, special) is lived out on the fantastic site of consumption. Pop music is a crucial source of imagined identities – in 'our' songs and singers (pop is always a matter of possession) we recognize, as if for the first time, our own desires – and in Britain art school musicians have given this pop role an unusual self-consciousness. They are, after all, experts in the intricacies of such 'imaging', and have both drawn on and made more sophisticated the British ability to use style to register the nuances of class, the ambiguities of sex, the differences of race. And here lies the clue to our starting puzzle: why have art schools been so important for British pop (and British pop so important for world-wide entertainment)? Because our continuing social rigidity (the sparse opportunities for higher education, the limits on social and geographical mobility) and our increasing marginality (Britain is essentially a suburban not a metropolitan society) mean that the handling of success and failure, ambition and dismay, are ever more dependent on the right accent, the right taste, the right cut, on the proliferation of images of ourselves in other settings altogether.

Late May, 1986: A cold wet evening and style reporter Steven Dixon is in York, watching the weekend action. 'There they were, stepping off the buses that had brought them in from the surrounding council estates and suburbs, groups of teen 'n' twenty funsters out for the ritual pub crawl.' All of them dressed for the sun.

These boys were strutting about in light, white, thin cotton trousers either cut or rolled up to just below the calf. They were displaying a good five inches of bare leg twixt their trouser bottoms and the flimsy black Chinese slippers that they wore on sockless feet. Bright pastel-coloured vests and t-shirts covered their torsos. None of them were carrying pullovers or jackets. . . . The girls were even less well equipped to face the harsh environment. Again they wore white cotton jeans, so thin that you could clearly see their tiny white knickers through the material. Again the jeans were cut short and finished at mid-calf. Some wore

181

boxer shorts. Their pink, yellow or turquoise vests were slashed Madonna style to expose their midriffs. To complete the loose 'n' relaxed beach-girl image their vests were worn with one strap hanging down so that a shoulder was provocatively unadorned.[35]

Dixon watched a couple arrive as if from a Bounty Bar or Martini ad, a windsurf board and sail on the roof rack of their car, and he noticed what made it all real for them: the TAN. The tan courtesy of the sun-bed. No one here had been on a winter break (this is the Tebbit generation); they'd bought their look across the counter of the hairdresser, the beauty parlour and the keep-fit centre. And so every weekend they gather in dreary, drizzly York and Birmingham and Crewe and act not as if they were on holiday but as if they were in an advertisement for holidays. Shivering. A simulation, but for real.

NOTES

1 Art and pop

1 Dick Hebdige (1979) *Subculture*, Methuen, London. This approach was briefly influential in the *New Musical Express* too – in the early 1980s Ian Penman and Paul Morley carved out a poststructuralist journalistic space for themselves: pop-critic-as-true-artist!

2 For an intriguing attempt to both sustain *and* disrupt this myth see Paul Morley's collection of *NME* interviews (1986) *Ask*, Faber & Faber, London.

3 Howard S. Becker (1980) *Art Worlds*, University of California Press, Los Angeles. H. Stith Bennett (1980) *On Becoming a Rock Musician*, University of Massachussetts Press, Amherst.

4 John Rockwell, 'Art rock' in Jim Miller (ed.) (1980) *The Rolling Stone Illustrated History of Rock & Roll*, Random House, New York, p.347.

5 By far the best summary account of the concept is Andreas Huyssen (1984): 'Mapping the postmodern', *New German Critique* 34.

6 Fredric Jameson, 'Foreword' to Jean-François Lyotard (1984) *The Postmodern Condition*, Manchester University Press, Manchester, p.vii.

7 Perry Anderson (1984) 'Modernity and revolution', *New Left Review* 144, p.106.

8 Fredric Jameson, 'Postmodernism and consumer society' in Hal Foster (ed.) (1985) *Postmodern Culture*, Pluto, London, p.124.

9 Jameson in Foster, op. cit., p.118 and see Anderson, op. cit., p.107 and Dick Hebdige (1985) 'The bottom line on Planet One', *Ten. 8* 18, p.42.

10 Lyotard, op. cit., p.76.

11 Marshall Berman (1982) *All That Is Solid Melts Into Air*, Simon & Schuster, New York, p.169. 'The signs in the street' is the title of his reply to Perry Anderson in *New Left Review* 144, and see Susan Buck-Morss (1983) 'Benjamin's *Passagen-Werk*: redeeming mass culture for the revolution', *New German Critique* 29, p.214. For the latest exponent of the *flâneur* approach see Iain Chambers (1985) *Urban Rhythms*, Macmillan, London; and (1986) *Popular Culture*, Methuen, London. Chambers finds hope in the subcultural reworking of commercial sign language but this still seems a somewhat arbitrary process.

12 C. Carr (1985) 'Money changes everything. The East Village art mart', *Voice Literary Supplement*, September, p.7. The following year, in the same neighbourhood, Steven Spielberg knocked down a tenement in order to build a Hollywood model of a tenement.

13 Peter Fuller (1981) 'The crisis of professionalism in art', *International*, July, p.30; Robert Hughes (1980) *The Shock of the New*, BBC Publications, London, p.324.

14 John A. Walker (1983) *Art in the Age of Mass Media*, Pluto, London, p.78.

15 Quoted in Jon Savage (1983) 'Guerilla Graphics: the tactics of Agit Pop art', *The Face* 42.

16 Warren I. Susman (1984) *Culture as History*, Pantheon, New York, p.189.

17 Richard Hamilton (1982) *Collected Words*, Thames & Hudson, London, p.78.

18 See Jean Baudrillard (1985) 'The ecstasy of communication' in Foster, op. cit., p.127.

19 For an important discussion of these points see Tania Modleski 'A feminist approach to mass culture' in Colin MacCabe (ed.) (1986) *High Theory/ Low Culture*, Manchester University Press, Manchester, pp.47–8, from where the quotations come.

20 Rosalind H. Williams (1982) *Dream Worlds*, University of California Press, Berkeley, p.67. And see Buck-Morss, op. cit., p.232.

21 ibid., p.110.

22 Roy McMullen (1968) *Art, Affluence and Alienation*, Pall Mall Press, London, p.41. And see Rachel Bowlby (1985) *Just Looking: Consumer Culture in Dreiser, Gissing and Zola*, Methuen, London, p.8.

23 Hamilton, op. cit., p.141; McMullen, op. cit., p.190.

24 Hamilton, op. cit., pp.143–4. And see Adrian Forty (1986) *Objects of Desire: Design and Society from Wedgwood to IBM*, Pantheon, New York, p.7. For Hamilton, as for other 1950s commentators on industrial design, cars and their consumers were the most interesting 'shaped' objects, and so it is instructive to note a contemporary spread in *Autocar* on the Italian styling firm Ital Design (responsible for the Lotus Esprit and BMW M1, the Fiat Uno and Panda, as well as Seiko watches, Nikon cameras and a new type of pasta!). The head of styling, Giorgio Giugiaro, comments that 'working on cars was not a choice, but

something which happened. I started work with cars, so it was a way to use my creativity. I would have liked to be an artist, instead I am a sculptor of mass production cars.' (*Autocar*, 9 April 1986, p.36.)

25 K. Marx and F. Engels (1976) *On Literature and Art*, Progress, Moscow, p.129.
26 Dave Laing (1985) *One Chord Wonders: Power and Meaning in Punk Rock*, Open University Press, Milton Keynes, p.19.
27 Hamilton, op. cit., p.151.
28 See Susman, op. cit., chapter 14.
29 Cotton master quoted in Forty, op. cit., p.90.
30 Maxine Berg (1985) *The Age of Manufactures, 1700–1820*, Fontana, London, p.172.
31 Elizabeth Wilson (1985) *Adorned in Dreams*, Virago, London, p.60.
32 Bowlby, op. cit., p.20; Janet Wolff (1985) 'The invisible *flâneuse*: women and the literature of modernity', *Theory, Culture and Society* 2 (3), p.44; and see Ann Cullis (1985) 'Going public: women using city spaces', *Feminist Art News* 2 (3), pp.14–16.
33 See Fred and Judy Vermorel (1985) *Starlust*, W.H. Allen, London.
34 Derek Jarman (1984) *Dancing Ledge*, Quartet, London, p.164.
35 Simon Frith, 'Art ideology and pop practice' in C. Nelson and L. Grossberg (eds) (1987) *Marxism and the Interpretation of Culture*, University of Illinois Press, Urbana, pp. 461–2.
36 Gramsci is quoted in Craig McGregor (1983) *Pop Goes the Culture*, Pluto, London, p.iv. And see Peter Bürger (1984) *Theory of the Avant-Garde*, University of Minnesota Press, Minneapolis, p.98.
37 Paul Morley (1984) *Blitz* 26, November.
38 Hal Foster (1984) '(Post) Modern polemics', *New German Critique* 33, p.76; Walker, op. cit., pp.51–2.
39 Quoted in Anthony Korner (1986) 'Aurora Musicalis', *Artforum* XXIV (10), p.79.
40 Huyssen, op. cit., p.48.
41 Berman, op. cit., p.345.
42 Richard Barnes (1979) *Mods!*, Eel Pie, London, p.6.

2 The art school context

1 Pete Frame (1983) *Rock Family Trees*, vol. 2, Omnibus, London, p.19. This is a comment on a tree called 'The art school dance goes on forever', tracing the history of the 1970s Hornsey College scene, and featuring Art Attacks, Adam Ant, Wire, the Vibrators, Monochrome Set, Models, etc.
2 Quoted in Al Clark (ed.) (1982) *The Rock Yearbook 1983*, Virgin Books, London, p.228.
3 Quoted in *The Face* 22, 1982, p.43.
4 Where published sources are not cited quotes come from our own interviews.

5 Paul Convery, quoted in K. Baynes (ed.) (1983) *Young Blood: Britain's Design Schools Today and Tomorrow*, Design in Industry/Lund Humphries, London, p.45.

6 *Blitz* 12, June 1983, p.28.

7 The USA is a good example for comparison. Although similar issues of ideology and practice run through American art colleges – there are the same distinctions between fine and applied arts, the same career pressures and limitations – American art schools tend to be more structured. The first 'real' art school in the States, Massachussetts State Normal Art School, opened in 1873, was modelled on the London School of Design. American art schools are still more obviously organized around technical needs than the British – in Stuart Macdonald's words, they 'are still far more closely related to industry and commerce than their British and French counterparts'. Students in the USA are more likely to attend college in or near their home town; part of the romance of the British art school, after the foundation year at least, is the flight from home to 'the city', from the provincial to the prestigious course. The major difference, though, is the relationship of the art school to the wider art world – in Britain, this is much more direct. See Stuart Macdonald (1970) *The History and Philosophy of Art Education*, University of London Press, London, p.261; A. Strauss, 'The art school and its students' in Albrecht, Barnett and Griff (eds) (1970) *The Sociology of Art and Literature*, Duckworth, London; J.E. Adler (1979) *Artists in Offices: An Ethnography of an Academic Art Scene*, Transaction Books, New Brunswick, NY.

8 Terry Atkinson (1984) 'Fredric Jameson's "The cultural logic of capitalism" ', *AND (Journal of Art and Art Education)* 3/4, p.6.

9 The first English art school as such was the Royal Academy Schools of Design. Founded in 1768, the RA Schools was a self-financing enterprise, free of state and commercial patronage. Under the despotic guidance of Sir Joshua Reynolds (and the personal patronage of George III), the Schools studiously ignored the realities of trade and art's possible commercial responsibilities, and gloried in the status of a finishing school of high culture: a comfortable haven where young middle-class men could pass happy and industrious hours copying antique relics and stylizing Life and Nature. This was in sharp contrast to art 'academies' in the rest of Europe which were precisely concerned to make art a commercial practice, answerable to the needs of manufacture.

10 Cited in C. Ashwin (1975) *Art Education: Documents and Sources 1768–1975*, Society for Research into Higher Education, London, p.12.

11 The practical model for the new schools was the science of design practised in Germany. From its inception, the state sector of British art and design education promoted a rigid orthodoxy, a slavish learning of practical and technical skills far removed from the fluid, elegant and decorative abilities encouraged by the French studio system and from

the classical aesthetics taught in the Royal Academy. The Academic concept of the 'professional fine artist' remained an anathema to the state training system throughout the nineteenth century. What was required was a concrete use value for artistic practice, a direct relevance for industry. Government regulations of 1843 made the point categorically: 'No person making Art his profession shall be eligible for admission as a student' to one of the new schools of design.

12 E. Fischer (1963) *The Necessity of Art*, Penguin, Harmondsworth, p.49.
13 P. Bürger (1984) *Theory of the Avant-Garde*, University of Minnesota Press, Minneapolis, p.46.
14 D. Judd (1985) 'A long discussion not about master-pieces but why there are so few of them', *Art Monthly* 83, February, p.3.
15 Quentin Bell remarked about the schools that, in 1852,

> The curriculum had nothing to do with aesthetic feeling, nothing to do with nature or the imagination; it was established not for the benefit of the pupils but for that of their prospective employers. (Quoted in J. Willett (1967) *Art in a City*, Methuen, London, p.226.)

This compares with Henry Cole's view of the system, delivered in a speech made shortly before his resignation from the Department of Science and Art in 1873:

> Since the year 1852, I have witnessed the conversion of twenty limp Schools of Design into one hundred and twenty flourishing Schools of Art in all parts of the United Kingdom, and other schools like them, in the Colonies and the United States. (Quoted in S. Macdonald, op. cit., p.222.)

Other training initiatives, like the Slade School, which opened in 1871, eschewed totally ideas of dogmatic pragmatism. The Slade system, innovatory in employing practising fine artists and in its emphasis on drawing skills, was to become a powerful influence on art school teaching.

16 Quoted in T. Hilton (1970) *The Pre-Raphaelites*, Thames & Hudson, London, p.135.
17 By the end of the nineteenth century, there was a general agreement within the art schools that threats of subservience could only be resisted by strengthening the definition of fine art as free practice. As Pevsner states: 'The academician was now wholly convinced that Schiller and the Romantic School had done right in establishing the sacredness of art' (N. Pevsner (1973) *Academies of Art Past and Present*, De Capo, New York, p.225).
18 G. Probert (1984) 'The boardroom', *AND* 3/4, p.44.
19 Roger Hilton (1985) *St Ives 1939–64: Twenty-Five Years of Painting, Sculpture and Pottery*, Tate Gallery, London.
20 Adrian Berg (1984) *The Hard Won Image*, Tate Gallery, London, p.35.

21 *Observer* magazine, 2 June 1985, p.15.

22 Elizabeth Wilson (1985) *Adorned in Dreams*, Virago, London, p.90.

23 The survey was carried out when the Dip. AD was still in force, before the general integration of graduate level qualifications into the CNAA. See C. Madge and B. Weinberger (1973) *Art Students Observed*, Faber & Faber, London, p.79.

24 Rosemary Burton (1977) 'Notes on teaching art', *Art Monthly* 6, p.17.

25 *Observer* magazine, 2 June 1985, p.14.

26 Initially strict and rigid in its operation, the NDD had only been in force for one year when the Committee on Art Examinations was formed to investigate ways of liberating procedures and to delegate course organization to individual institutions.

27 R. Macdonald (1985) 'Central's line to calamity', *Guardian*, 15 January, p.9.

28 David Halliwell (1967) *Little Malcolm and his Struggle against the Eunuchs*, Faber & Faber, London, p.22.

29 Quoted in Simon Frith (1981) *Sound Effects*, Pantheon, New York, p.76. And see Eric Burdon (1986) *I Used to be an Animal but I'm Alright Now*, Faber & Faber, London, p. 36.

30 Madge and Weinberger, op. cit., pp.28 and 33.

31 DES (1963) *Annual Review*, p.47.

32 T. Nairn and J. Singh-Sandhu, 'Chaos in the art colleges', in A.Cockburn and R. Blackburn (eds) (1969) *Student Power*, Penguin, Harmondsworth, p.104.

33 Comment from the original catalogue to the 1959 ICA exhibition, *The Developing Process*.

34 Quoted in R. Macdonald (1985) 'Painted into a corner', *Guardian*, 16 January, p.17.

35 *Observer* magazine, 2 June 1985, p.14.

36 Quoted in S. Macdonald, op. cit., p.358.

37 A. Ironside (1985) 'Art education and the technological media: is the tail wagging the dog?' *AND* 5, p.26.

38 Pru Branwell-Davies, quoted in *Sunday Times*, 14 July 1968.

39 J. Berger (1979) *Permanent Red*, Writers & Readers, London, p.51.

40 The most systematic attempt to discover who earns what from art was the Gulbenkian-sponsored inquiry into *The Economic Situation of the Visual Artist in the UK* which, though never formally published as a report, was placed in select art college libraries in 1986. For discussion of its findings see Philip Wright's summary in *Art Monthly* 93, April 1986 and N. Pearson's 'More on the economic situation of the visual artist', *Art Monthly* 95, June 1986. The report makes clear the dependence of practising artists on teaching income (and the dominance of the art teaching profession by men) and the pressure on postgraduate college courses (ten applicants per place), and implies that artists' dependence on state patronage – teaching jobs, Arts Council, Regional Arts and local authority exhibitions/commissions – helps

keep returns from art low. Only those artists exhibiting in the private sector have to develop skills of marketing, have to learn to build on success. But underlying all these arguments is the point that compared with other European countries, Britain simply produces too many would-be professional artists – approximately 3,100 art and design students graduated from universities and polytechnics in 1983.

41 G. Evans (1984) 'America, Britain and the art school', *AND* 1, p.31.
42 Quoted in K. Baynes, op. cit., p.44.
43 Hornsey students occupied the college buildings on 28 May 1968, Guildford students followed on 5 June and on 10 June, Birmingham students organized a boycott of first- and second-year history of art examinations.
44 This and the following quote are from Hornsey College of Art, Students and Staff (1969) *The Hornsey Affair*, Penguin, Harmondsworth, p.18.
45 ibid. p.64.
46 A student recalling the events of the summer of 1968, in a later edition of the Hornsey paper *Revelations*, stated:

> In the six weeks of the Hornsey Revolution I had more education than I had ever previously experienced. A new sort of freedom emerged, a freedom to work, learn and develop. A new surge of life. . . . We had freedom to express ourselves creatively and yet end our isolation from the world, the helplessness of the individual was at an end, we began to realise that art was revolutionary. (Quoted in David Widgery (1976) *The Left in Britain 1956–68*, Penguin, Harmondsworth, p. 332)

47 Jeff Nuttall (1970) *Bomb Culture*, Paladin, St Albans, p.161.
48 R. Neville (1971) *Playpower*, Paladin, St Albans, p.120.
49 ibid., pp.14–15.
50 Peter Marsh (1977) 'Dole queue rock', *New Society*, 20 January, p.114.
51 D. Hebdige (1979) *Subculture*, Methuen, London, pp.115–16.
52 *ZG* 7, no date, p.17.
53 P. Fuller (1980) *Beyond the Crisis in Art*, Writers & Readers, London, p.45.
54 R. Hughes (1980) *The Shock of the New*, BBC Publications, London, p.366.
55 Nuttall, op. cit., pp.119–20.
56 Hans Richter (1965) *Dada*, Thames & Hudson, London, p.50.
57 Bürger, op. cit., pp.xxxvi and 49–50.
58 H. Rosenberg (1973) *Discovering the Present*, University of Chicago Press, Chicago, p.xi.
59 G. Battcock (ed.) (1973) *The New Art*, Dutton, New York, p.21.
60 L. Alloway (1969) 'Popular culture and Pop art', *Studio International*, July/August. The blurring of distinctions was exemplified by

American Pop artist Claes Oldenberg, who recalled: 'In 1952 I declared that I was going to be an artist, but this seemed at the time a disguise. It gave me greater freedom than declaring I would be a newspaper man. In a way, a newspaper man is more what I really am' (quoted in G. Woods et al. (eds) (1972) *Art Without Boundaries*, Thames & Hudson, London, p.23).

61 *Working in Fine Arts* (1983), Careers and Occupational Information Centre, Manpower Services Commission, p.2. And see Burdon, op. cit., p.36.

62 M. Black, 'Notes on design education in Great Britain' in David Piper (ed.) (1973) *After Hornsey*, Davis-Poynter, London, p.31.

63 Quoted in *Designers at Work*, exhibition catalogue, Design Centre, 1985.

64 Quoted in K. Baynes, op. cit., p.24.

65 *Guardian*, 4 January 1985.

66 E. Lucie-Smith (1966) 'Pop and the mass audience', *Studio International*, August.

67 Deyan Sudjic (1986) 'How design grew to be big business,' *Blueprint* 28, June, pp.16, 18.

68 *Blitz* 26, November 1984, p.32. In the 1980s record companies have been significant employers of designers, like Malcolm Garrett of Assorted Images, who

> began designing album covers for local bands, like the Buzzcocks and Magazine, on his bedroom floor while he was still at college in Manchester. It was there he evolved his geometric/typographic style that has been emulated so often it has slipped insidiously into all the products of youth culture. (Alan Pipes (1985) 'Artificial images', *Design* 439, July, p.45)

Garrett pioneered the use of CAD (computer-aided design) in designing LP covers – c.f. his work for Electric Dreams.

69 *The Face* 57, January 1985, p.51.

3 The rock bohemians

1 Alison Fell, 'Rebel with a cause' in Liz Heron (ed.) (1985) *Truth, Dare or Promise*, Virago, London, p.24.

2 Jim Godbolt (1976) *All This and 10%*, Robert Hale, London, p.37. Humphrey Lyttelton (1954) *I Play as I Please*, Macgibbon and Kee, London, pp. 116–25. And see Jim Godbolt (1984) *A History of Jazz in Britain 1919–50*, Quartet, London, ch. 12.

3 Peter Blake (1985) 'Art into music', *Aspects* 31, Winter 1985/6, p.6.

4 Bob Brunning (1986) *Blues – The British Connection*, Blandford, Poole, p.60.

5 Francis Newton (1961) *The Jazz Scene*, Penguin, Harmondsworth, p.238.

NOTES

6 Iris Murdoch (1958) *The Bell*, Chatto & Windus, London, p.1; Mary Quant (1967) *Quant by Quant*, Pan, London, p.8.

7 Humphrey Lyttelton (1958) *Second Chorus*, MacGibbon & Kee, London, pp.24–5, 68, 71.

8 Paul Oliver (1957) 'Art aspiring', *Jazz Monthly* 2 (12), February, pp.2–3. George Melly, then a touring musician with Mick Mulligan's Band, suggests that 1950s jazz was 'the suburb's escape from their lot'. He too remembers the audiences as 'middle-class and suburban, with a strong element of students, particularly from art schools' (quoted in Peter Lewis (1978) *The 50s*, Heinemann, London, p.141).

9 Jeff Nuttall (1970) 'Techniques of separation', *Anatomy of Pop*, BBC Publications, London, p.113.

10 Newton, op. cit., p.223. Compare Howard Becker's famous (1963) study of 1950s white American jazz musicians, *Outsiders*, Free Press, New York, ch. 5.

11 ibid., pp.224, 229, 239–41.

12 George Melly (1970) *Revolt into Style*, Allen Lane, London, p.130.

13 See Melly, op. cit., p.147; Quant, op. cit, *passim*; and Elizabeth Wilson (1985) *Adorned in Dreams*, Virago, London, p.174.

14 Folk never seems to have had the art school appeal of jazz, so skiffle did act to bring the two worlds together, and Nancy Whiskey, for example, folk singer turned skiffle star, was a student at Glasgow School of Art. The phrase 'jazz cellar raciness' was Kenneth Allsop's.

15 Barbara Charone (1979) *Keith Richards*, Futura, London, p.24.

16 John Platt, Chris Dreja and Jim McCarty (1983) *Yardbirds*, Sidgwick & Jackson, London, p.8. John Lennon quote from Hunter Davies (1981) *The Beatles*, Panther, London, p.64.

17 Davies, op. cit., p.77 and Ray Coleman (1985) *John Lennon*, Futura, London, pp.62–3.

18 *Sounds*, 10 November 1981.

19 Stephen Davis (1985) *Hammer of the Gods*, Sidgwick & Jackson, London, p.18.

20 Dave Marsh (1983) *Before I Get Old*, St Martin's Press, New York, pp.50–1.

21 Philip Norman (1981) *Shout!*, Elm Tree, London, p.52. And see Eric Burdon (1986) *I Used to be an Animal but I'm Alright Now*, Faber & Faber, London, pp.17–19.

22 The best account of the Beatles' art school influences is Mike Evans (1984) *The Art of the Beatles*, Anthony Blond, London, ch. 1.

23 Norman, op. cit., p.52.

24 Platt et al., op. cit., p.12; The Rolling Stones (1964) *Our Own Story*, Corgi, London, p.25; Marsh, op. cit., p.95; Pete Frame (ed.) (1974) *The Road to Rock*, Charisma, London, p.24.

25 Platt et al., op. cit., p.21.

26 ibid., p.14.

27 Richard Barnes (1979) *Mods!*, Eel Pie, London, p.12.

28 The Rolling Stones, op. cit., p.187.

29 See John Pidgeon (1976) *Eric Clapton*, Panther, London, ch. 4, quote from p.65.

30 ibid., p.71.

31 H.L. Menken is quoted by Rachel Bowlby (1985) *Just Looking*, Methuen, London, p.124. And see Iain Chambers (1985) *Urban Rhythms*, Macmillan, London, p.61.

32 See Elizabeth Wilson (1982) *Mirror Writing*, Virago, London, pp.71–2.

33 Ray Davies interviewed by Nicky Horne on *Earsay*, Channel 4, 1 September 1984; Bryan Ferry interviewed by James Truman in *The Face*, 60, April 1985, p.47.

34 Interviewed by Simon Frith in 1986.

35 Charles Perry (1984) *The Haight-Ashbury*, Random House, New York, p.70. Cippollina quoted in Gene Sculatti and Davin Seay (1985) *San Francisco Nights*, Sidgwick & Jackson, London, p.91. This sort of art world – 'beat' culture plus 'folk' music – could be found on a smaller scale in most US cities. See, for example, Robert Shelton's description of 1960 Minneapolis in his biography of Bob Dylan (1986) *No Direction Home*, Hodder & Stoughton, London.

36 Terrazzo Brother John Cuff, quoted in Sculatti and Seay, op. cit., p.21.

37 Quoted in ibid., p.25.

38 Lenny Kaye (1985) 'Elektrorock – the sixties' (sleevenotes to the Elektra record of that title), p.5. And see Perry, op. cit., pp.63–9 and Sculatti and Seay, op. cit., pp.103–8.

39 Roger Waters quoted in Michael Wale (1972) *Vox Pop*, Harrap, London, pp.134–5.

40 John A. Walker (1984) 'Pop music: the art school connection', *Theatrephile*, 1(2) March, p. 71. And for an excellent tracing of 'underground' connections see Robert Hewison (1986) *Too Much*, Methuen, London, ch.3.

41 See the Pete Jenner and Pink Floyd interviews in Pete Frame (ed.) (1974) *The Road to Rock*, Charisma, London.

42 Sculatti and Seay, op. cit., p. 125.

43 Jeff Nuttall (1970) *Bomb Culture*, Paladin, London, pp. 120-2.

44 Quoted in Dave Marsh (1983) *Before I Get Old*, St Martin's Press, New York, p. 170.

45 Philip Norman (1984) *The Stones*, Elm Tree, London, p. 76; and see Quant, op. cit., p. 104.

46 Norman, *The Stones*, p. 97.

47 Richard Hamilton (1982) *Collected Words*, Thames & Hudson, London, p. 28.

48 Quoted in Lucy Lippard (1966) *Pop Art*, Thames & Hudson, London, p. 27.

49 Lawrence Alloway (1969) 'Popular culture and pop art', *Studio International*, July/August, p. 19.

50 Hamilton, op. cit., pp. 104–5. In the pop world, ironically, the Beatles'

white cover was taken to mark their move from art back to the 'new simplicity' called for in Dylan's *John Wesley Harding*.

51 Christine Perfect, to give one example, comments that 'I left art college with a diploma in sculpture, which was virtually worthless in the cold commercial world – so I came to London and worked as a window dresser . . . spent the next twelve months crawling around windows and looking at the legs of people shuffling down Regent Street.' It's not surprising she jumped at the chance to join Chicken Shack. Quoted in Pete Frame (1980) *Rock Family Trees*, Omnibus, London, p. 12.

52 Melly, op. cit., pp. 133-4.

53 Dick Hebdige (1983) 'In poor taste', *Block* 8, p. 56.

54 David Mellor (1983) 'David Bailey 1961-66' in *David Bailey*, V & A exhibition catalogue, p. 7; Hebdige, op. cit., p. 58.

55 Andy Warhol and Pat Hackett (1980) *POPism The Warhol '60s*, Harcourt Brace Jovanovich, New York, pp. 3-4.

56 ibid., pp. 20-1.

57 Interviewed by William Shaw in *Blitz* 30, April 1985.

58 Morse Peckham (1970) *The Triumph of Romanticism: Collected Essays*, University of South Carolina Press, Columbia SC, pp. 236-7.

59 Viva (1972) *Superstar*, Sphere, London, p. 99; Warhol quoted in Victor Bockris and Gerard Malanga (1983) *Up-Tight The Velvet Underground Story*, Omnibus, London, p. 25.

60 Quotes from ibid., p. 25 (Malanga); Ralph J. Gleason (1969) *The Jefferson Airplane and the San Francisco Sound*, Ballantine, New York, p. 35; Robbie Woliver (1986) *Bringing It All Back Home*, Pantheon, New York, p. 134 (Van Ronk).

61 Bockris and Malanga, op. cit., p. 35.

62 ibid., p. 26.

63 Woliver, op. cit., p. 184.

64 ibid., p. 191.

65 Iggy Pop and Anne Wehrer (1982) *I Need More*, Karz–Cohl, Princeton, NY, p. 7.

66 John Rockwell (1983) *All American Music*, Knopf, New York, pp. 237-8.

67 Quoted in *The Face* 37, May 1983, p. 17.

68 Quoted in David Buxton (1985) *Le Rock*, La Pensée Sauvage, Paris, p. 198 (our translation). And see Walker, op. cit., p. 71.

69 Eno and Mills (1986) *More Dark Than Shark*, Faber & Faber, London, p. 40.

70 ibid., p. 41.

71 ibid., p. 101.

72 ibid., p. 44.

73 Private communication, 16 May 1982.

74 Robert Hughes (1980) *The Shock of the New*, BBC Publications, London, p. 379; and see Adrian Henri (1974) *Environments and Happenings*, Thames & Hudson, London, pp. 149-50.

75 John Rockwell, 'The sound of Manhattan' in Jim Miller (ed.) (1980) *The Rolling Stone Illustrated History of Rock & Roll*, Random House, New York, p. 352.

76 Andreas Huyssen (1975) 'The cultural politics of Pop: reception and critique of US Pop art in the Federal Republic of Germany', *New German Critique* 4, pp. 77-92; and see Hughes, op. cit., pp. 379-83. Beuys's interest in process obviously echoes Eno's concerns, and his interest in 'anthropology' (the activities of so-called 'primitive' peoples) and what we might call spontaneous creativity, was paralleled in 1970s Britain by developments in the improvised music scene. By the early 1970s experimental musicians in the art music/jazz scene were as likely to come from art as music colleges (Mike Westbrook, for example, had been an art student and Evan Parker studied at the RCA) and the London Musicians' Cooperative (founded in 1970) increasingly took on the atmosphere of an art college event. For the new generation of experimental art school musicians, like David Toop and David Cunningham, the aim was to combine commitments to free improvisation, recording technology, and an ethnomusicology of found sound. For these musicians, as for Beuys's students in Germany, it was punk rather than 'art rock' as such that was the significant pop movement – by the 1980s David Cunningham had had chart success with the Flying Lizards while Toop was the record columnist for *The Face*, and an expert on rap and other 'ethnic' pop sounds. Both had become successful record producers – as Cunningham told *ZG*, 'It's like the job of a graphic designer; shaping the idea into a product.' (*ZG* 1, 1981). And compare the career of Robin Scott (ex-Croydon) who moved from pop success as M to recording Kenyan music.

77 Anthony Fawcett and Joan Withers (1983) 'Beuys adventures', *The Face* 40, August, p. 51.

78 Hewison, op. cit., p. 141.

4 The pop situationists

1 Caroline Coon (1977) *1988: The New Wave Punk Rock Explosion*, Omnibus, London, p. 77.

2 Kathy Myers (1986) 'Hard lines', *City Limits*, 26 June, p. 12.

3 Quoted in Simon Garfield (1986) *Expensive Habits*, Faber & Faber, London, p. 244.

4 Dave Laing (1985) *One Chord Wonders*, Open University Press, Milton Keynes, pp. 121-2; Peter York (1980) *Style Wars*, Sidgwick & Jackson, London, p. 195.

5 The most illuminating sources of how careers and influences work in the music business are Pete Frame's *Rock Family Trees*. Here we've used volume 2, Omnibus, London, 1983.

We haven't attempted to list every art school musician in this book. Some (Lynsey de Paul, Gilbert O'Sullivan) don't fit our argument!

Others are still emerging after years in unsuccessful bands (John Campbell of It's Immaterial, Mick Hucknall of Simply Red, Bill Carter of Screaming Blue Messiahs, etc). There's also the interesting case of Holly Johnson, an *almost* art student. Johnson explained to Alix Sharkey why he hated his secondary school, Liverpool Collegiate:

> It was the kind of school that I felt that – say, to take the subject art, they thought art was for the people who they considered to be 'not bright' and this is a very British attitude towards art. It was for the people in the C and D streams and if you were in the A and B streams you didn't take art, you took a second language . . . British people don't take art seriously really. They think academic achievement is the be all and end all . . . they send girls to art school till they get married you know.

In the event he did get a place at Liverpool College, on the Foundation Course, but the band he was then in took off 'so I couldn't go which was a bit of a drag really 'cos I really *wanted* to go' ('It's Holly and Holly only', *i-D* 40, September 1986, p. 66).

6 Quotes from Frame, op. cit., p. 21 (Wylie); *Melody Maker*, 2 August 1986, p. 19 (Mindwarp); Mike West (1982) *Siouxsie and the Banshees*, Babylon Books, Manchester, p. 5 (Siouxsie); Dave Rimmer (1985) *Like Punk Never Happened*, Faber & Faber, London, pp. 17-18 (Green).

7 M. Fish and D. Hallbery (1985) *Cabaret Voltaire*, Serious Art Forms, Harrow, p. 39.

8 ibid., p. 33.

9 Fred and Judy Vermorel (1981) *Sex Pistols*, Star, London, p. 260.

10 Jon Savage, 'The new hippies' in Ian Birch (ed.) (1981) *The Book With No Name*, Omnibus, London, p. 40; and see Vermorels, op. cit., p. 270.

11 Vermorels, op. cit., pp. 273-4. In the mid-1960s the situationist paper *Heatwave*, edited by Chris Grey, was making counter-cultural points on the relationship of work and leisure, on the 'total revolution of life', and pioneering the photo-montage technique copied most successfully by *Oz*. Its successor, *King Mob Echo*, was the mouthpiece of London's King Mob. Formed around Grey and art college lecturers Dave and Stewart Wise, King Mob was dedicated to championing, in Fred Vermorel's words, 'anti-cultural activities like smashing up Wimpy Bars, defacing the work of lickarse artists, and publicly celebrating Valerie Solanas' shooting of Andy Warhol.' *King Mob Echo*, quoting Raoul Vaneigem, made familiar points about art and society, praising the Dadaists' attitude of 'contempt for art and bourgeois values', and advocating 'the same refusal of ideology, the same will to live'.

12 Jon Savage (1983) 'Guerilla graphics: the tactics of Agit Pop art', *The Face* 42, 1983. Reid also points out the technical trial and error involved in the Pistols' project – 'because you can do the most immaculate drawing that's a brilliant image, that won't print; yet you can take something supposedly as unsophisticated as the 'Anarchy' flag or 'God

Save the Queen' and you just know because of the print techniques that it'll work as an image, a very strong image.'

13 Laing, op. cit., p. 103; Tim Carr of the *New York Rocker* quoted in Billy Bergman and Richard Horn (1985) *Experimental Pop*, Blandford, Poole, p. 33; San Francisco details from Peter Belsito and Bob Davis (1983) *Hardcore California*, The Last Gasp of San Francisco, Berkeley, p. 107.

14 Fish and Hallbury, op. cit., p. 12 (our italics).

15 Quoted in Vermorels, op. cit., pp. 216-17.

16 Quoted in ibid., p. 152.

17 Alan Joyce (1980) 'Factory Records', *ZG* 1, p. 15.

18 Laing, op. cit., pp. 118-20.

19 Quoted in *i-D* 33, February 1986, p. 12.

20 York, op. cit., p. 114.

21 Rosetta Brooks (1980) 'Blitz culture', *ZG* 1; Rimmer, op. cit., pp. 19-21.

22 See Robert Hewison (1986) *Too Much*, Methuen, London, p. 242. Richard Butler, later to form the Psychedelic Furs, was a member of the Pose Band while Maclean's student – see his interview in *i-D*, April 1987.

23 Rimmer, op. cit., p. 22.

24 Quoted in Hugh Thompson (1985) 'The great style steal', *Guardian*, 2 December, p. 13; and see Adam Sweeting (1985) 'Style Council', *Guardian*, 2 September, p. 13.

25 Lester Bangs (1980) *Blondie*, Omnibus, London, pp. 65-6.

26 Jon Stratton, 'Capitalism and romantic ideology in the record business' in R. Middleton and D. Horn (eds) (1983) *Popular Music* 3, Cambridge University Press, Cambridge, p. 156.

27 See Simon Frith, 'Art ideology and pop practice' in C. Nelson and L. Grossberg (eds) (1987) *Marxism and the Interpretation of Culture*, University of Illinois Press, Champaign–Urbana.

28 Hipgnosis and R. Dean (eds) (1977) *The Album Cover Album, vol. 1*, Dragon's World, Limpsfield, Surrey, p. 15.

29 Quoted in Victoria Balfour (1986) *Rock Wives*, Beech Tree Books, New York, p. 137.

30 For this shift see Cynthia Rose, 'Worn out: career chic' in T. Stewart (ed.) (1981) *Cool Cats*, Eel Pie, London.

31 Hipgnosis and Dean, op. cit., p. 15.

32 Judith Williamson (1986) 'A piece of the action' in her *Consuming Passions*, Marion Boyars, London, p. 92. And see pp. 102, 112, The quote is from J.L. Baudry.

5 Art and pop revisited

1 Stephen Fay (1986) 'The pursuit of pop perfection', *Sunday Times Magazine*, 25 August, p. 41.

2 Undated press release from OUT Promotions.

3 And that musical equipment manufacturers like Yamaha are a possible

NOTES

source of funds. See Frank Owen (1986) 'Art pop', *i-D* 40, September.

4 As an editorial in *Art Monthly* 97 (June 1986) pointed out, the documentation of the effects of the cuts on art education is patchy and dependent on individual colleges' own ability/willingness to get publicity. For the typical fine art response to the situation see Patrick Heron's 'Benighted stupidity: the art school murdered' in *Art Monthly* 92, Dec./Jan. 1986 and note John A. Walker's comment in the following issue.

5 W.F. Haug (1986) *Critique of Commodity Aesthetics*, Polity, Cambridge, pp. 16-17.

6 Laura Kipnis, '"Refunctioning" reconsidered: towards a left popular culture' in Colin MacCabe (ed.) (1986) *High Theory/Low Culture*, Manchester University Press, Manchester, p. 27. And see Judith Williamson (1986) *Consuming Passions*, Marion Boyars, London p. 11.

7 For scathing comments on this see Andrew Brighton, 'Ill-education through art' and Peter Fuller, 'Art education: some observations' in *Aspects*, 18, 1982.

8 Scott Lash and John Urry (1987) *The End of Organised Capitalism*, Polity, Cambridge, ch. 10; Iain Chambers (1986) *Popular Culture*, Methuen, London, pp. 216-17. And see Susan Buck-Morss (1983) 'Benjamin's *Passagen-Werk*: redeeming mass culture for the revolution', *New German Critique* 29, p. 213.

9 See Todd Gitlin, '"We build excitement"' in Todd Gitlin (ed.) (1987) *Watching TV*, Pantheon, New York, p. 157.

10 *Journal of Communication Inquiry* 10 (1), Winter 1986, pp. 2, 74-5. John Fiske's 'MTV: post-structural post-modern' is, without a doubt, the silliest article on the subject so far, but even shrewder commentators in this vein, like E. Ann Kaplan (who appreciates that MTV is an advertising medium) interpret rock videos by reference to the tension between 'a potentially disruptive form, critical of bourgeois hegemony', and the 'commercializing' practices of MTV, as if rock weren't itself a commercial form, and as if *all* advertisements didn't play on the disruptive qualities of desire. The sleight of hand – what's taken to make rock videos a new sort of commercial – is the equation of subcultural resistance with the anarchy of signs. For an example of Kaplan's work see 'A postmodern play of the signifier? Advertising, pastiche and schizophrenia in music television' in P. Drummond and R. Paterson (eds) (1986) *Television in Transition*, BFI, London, pp. 146-63. See also her (1987) *Rocking Around the Clock*, Methuen, London.

11 Quoted in *The Face* 45, January 1984, p. 70.

12 Jody Berland (1985-6) 'Sound, image and the media', *Parachute* 41, p. 17.

13 Pop videos are almost all funded and designed by record companies' promotion departments, and, in the end, video-makers, like advertising agencies, are answerable to their clients' briefs (Art of Noise were then signed to ZTT).

14 Pat Aufderheide 'The look of the sound' in Gitlin, op. cit., pp. 133-4. For further analysis from this perspective see Mark Hustwitt (1985)

Sure Feels Like Heaven To Me, IASPM Working Paper 6; Deborah E. Holdstein (1984) 'Music video: messages and structure', *Jump/Cut* 29; Marsha Kinder (1984) 'Music video and the spectator', *Film Quarterly* 38 (1), Fall.

15 For Jameson, Baudrillard and Chambers see the references in chapter 1. For Grossberg see, for example, 'I'd rather feel bad than not feel anything: rock & roll, pleasure & power', *enclitic* 6, 1984.

16 Thomas Lawson (1981) 'Last exit: painting', *Artforum* 20 (2) p. 451. And see Rosalind Krauss (1981) 'The originality of the avant-garde: a postmodernist repetition', *October* 18, p. 66.

17 Robert Hughes (1982) 'The rise of Andy Warhol', *New York Review of Books*, 18 February, p.6. And see Fred and Judy Vermorel (1985) *Starlust*, Comet, London.

18 Michael Musto (1986) *Downtown*, Vintage, New York, pp. 107, 113.

19 Teresa De Lauretis (1984) *Alice Doesn't*, Indiana University Press, Bloomington, pp. 38–44.

20 For an important version of this argument see David Buxton (1985) *Le Rock: Star-Système et Société de Consommation*, La Pensée Sauvage, Grenoble.

21 See Georgina Born (1987) 'Modernism, the popular and post-modernism', *New Formations* 2.

22 For an expanded version of this argument see Simon Frith (1986) 'Art versus technology: the strange case of popular music', *Media Culture and Society* 8 (3), pp. 263–80.

23 Fuller, op. cit., p. 13.

24 Chris Cutler (1986) 'Skill – the negative case for some new music technology', *The Re Records Quarterly* 3, p. 25.

25 ibid., p. 27.

26 Eno quotes from Anthony Korner (1986) 'Aurora Musicalis', *Artforum*, 24 (10), Summer, pp. 76–9.

27 Quoted in *The Face* 78, October 1986, p. 42.

28 Angela McRobbie (1986) 'Postmodernism and popular culture', *ICA Documents 5, Postmodernism*, ICA, London, p. 58 and see Andreas Huyssen (1984) 'Mapping the postmodern', *New German Critique* 34, pp. 49–50. But note that Lash and Urry, following Bourdieu, find the postmodern audience in the new service-sector petit bourgeoisie, while Gitlin refers approvingly to Fred Pfeil's thesis that postmodern culture is yuppie culture.

29 Jeff Nuttall (1980) 'Bubble-pack culture', *Guardian*, 12 January, p.9.

30 Philip Norman (1986) 'The age of parody', *Sunday Times*, 5 January, p. 35.

31 Simon Reynolds (1986) 'Ladybirds and Start-Rite Kids', *Melody Maker*, 27 September, p. 45.

32 ibid., p. 44.

33 Quoted in David Sharman (1986) 'Across the bored', *Sunday Express Magazine*, 14 September, p. 25.

34 Jamie Reid and Jon Savage (1987) *Up They Rise*, Faber & Faber, p. 15.

35 Steven Dixon (1986) 'Sun-bed kids', *i-D* 40, September, p. 84.

INDEX

INDEX